COIN *of the* YEAR

Celebrating Three Decades of the Best in Coin Design and Craftsmanship

DONALD SCARINCI

Published by

Krause Publications, a division of F+W, A Content + eCommerce Company
700 East State Street • Iola, WI 54990-0001
715-445-2214 • 888-457-2873
www.krausebooks.com

To order books or other products call toll-free 1-800-258-0929
or visit us online at www.shopnumismaster.com

ISBN-13: 978-1-4402-4476-6
ISBN-10: 1-4402-4476-6

Designed by Sharon Bartsch
Edited by Paul Kennedy and Thomas Michael

Printed in China

Contents

INTRODUCTION..4

1984 AWARDS 6
1985 AWARDS 9
1986 AWARDS 12
1987 AWARDS.................... 15
1988 AWARDS 18
1989 AWARDS 21
1990 AWARDS 24
1991 AWARDS....................28
1992 AWARDS....................31
1993 AWARDS 34
1994 AWARDS 37
1995 AWARDS 41
1996 AWARDS 45
1997 AWARDS....................49
1998 AWARDS 53
1999 AWARDS 57

2000 AWARDS 61
2001 AWARDS....................65
2002 AWARDS 69
2003 AWARDS 73
2004 AWARDS 77
2005 AWARDS 81
2006 AWARDS 85
2007 AWARDS 89
2008 AWARDS 93
2009 AWARDS 98
2010 AWARDS.................... 102
2011 AWARDS.................... 106
2012 AWARDS.................... 110
2013 AWARDS....................115
2014 AWARDS.................... 120
2015 AWARDS.................... 125

ABOUT THE AUTHOR.............................. 130
INDEX.. 131

A Celebration of Achievement

By Donald Scarinci

An award for excellence in coinage design first issued in 1984 by Krause Publications in Iola, Wisconsin, has become the ultimate international recognition of mints and their artists, growing into the community's most coveted award for contemporary world coins.

Today, artists and mints worldwide openly compete for one of the Krause Coin of the Year categories. The announcement of the Coin of the Year is one of the highlights of the annual World Money Fair, and the winner is internationally celebrated. Any remaining mintage of the winner quickly sells out and coin values rise dramatically on the secondary market. This is, indeed, solid evidence of the global acceptance, standing and success of the annual award.

The Coin of the Year Award had a humble origin as a pet project of Krause Publications' founder Chester "Chet" Krause and former Krause Publications' President and CEO Clifford "Cliff" Mishler. By highlighting medallic art with merit, Mishler hoped to encourage world mints to improve the art of coins. Few could have imagined how the brainchild of these two pioneering men would be so well received today.

An international panel of judges nominates and votes for coins in each category. Category winners then compete for the grand prize—the Krause Coin of the Year.

The first award in 1984 began a tradition of honoring coins that were minted two years prior to the ceremony. Thus, the inaugural Coin of the Year went to the United States Mint for Elizabeth Jones' 1982 design of the George Washington Commemorative half dollar. This inspiring design, commemorating the 250th anniversary of the birth of George Washington, was the first commemorative coin issued in the United States since 1954, when the previous program was suspended.

The United States and Canada were the first winners, causing concern that the award would be myopic in focus, gazing only at the design work done in North America. Those fears were set aside when Finland won the award in 1987 for its 1985 design, "Kalevala National Epic." This was the first time a coin with what could be considered a modernist design was selected for international recognition by the Krause judges.

By 1990, with the Coin of the Year going to Albania for its 1988 dated silver 50-Leke "Railroads" design, the prestigious award began to gain acceptance as an international award. The 50-Leke is a five-ounce silver round with a piercing that invites the viewer to follow the path of a train as it goes through a tunnel. With the coin's selection, the Krause judges made it clear they viewed coins as three-dimensional objects, not merely pretty pictures on metal. The award to Albania in 1990 validated the Coin of the Year as a truly international award of merit for innovation and artistic excellence in world coins.

When the award began, an overall Coin of the Year was selected as well as six category winners: Most Popular; Most Historically Significant; Most Artistic; Best Gold Coin; Best Silver Coin; and Best Crown. Through the years, as the competition evolved, other categories were added – and some removed – to bring the total number of judged categories to ten. The later categories were: Most Inspirational; Best Contemporary Event (defined as an event within the last 100 years); Most Innovative; Best Bi-Metallic; and Best Circulating.

As interest in the Coin of the Year has surged, a fascinating offshoot of the program has emerged – collecting the winning coins. I've found collecting Coin of the Year coins a rewarding experience. Assembling a collection of the main winners is challenging enough to be fun; but, with the exception of the gold and platinum issues, the winning coins are not excessively expensive to collect. Some have small mintages, but that does not translate into big price tags.

Selecting a category like Most Historical, where Krause defines "historical" as the passage of at least 100 years, is like taking a survey class in world history from the point of view of the coin-issuing country. A coin like the 1986 dated Austria 500-Schilling, commemorating the 500th anniversary of the first dollar with a set of coins from each of the six current mints, is a wonderful gateway to study the origin and history of the dollar denomination around the world.

A quick scan of the topics chosen by coin-issuing authorities expands your perception of what a country considers to be its important events, or of its contributions to the world, such as the 1995 German 10 Mark commemorative for the 100th anniversary of the X-ray. The 2003 Australia silver 10 Dollar "Evolution of the Alphabet" coin is a fascinating piece and a wonderfully curious subject for that country to choose.

A collection of the Most Inspirational would begin with the 1993 Poland 300,000 Zlotych, which marked the Warsaw Ghetto Uprising. The coins that have received this award range from the 1996 Paralympics silver dollar from the United States to the 2006 Pink Ribbon 25-cent coin from the Royal Canadian Mint, struck to raise breast cancer awareness.

The Best Contemporary Event category, added in 1996 with the award for the 1994 United Kingdom 50 Pence commemorating the 50th Anniversary of the Invasion of Normandy, is a wonderful way to study more modern history. These coins remind us of the ancient Greek and Roman practice of using coins as the newspapers of their day, communicating a message or persuading the public of the benefit of a leader, event or building.

A collection of these coins includes subjects ranging from the 1997 South Africa 1 Rand honoring the first heart transplant to the 2000 German 10 Mark celebrating the 10th Anniversary of the German reunification. These coins are as interesting for their designs as they are for the topics they commemorate.

Perhaps my favorite category is Most Innovative. As a group, these coins show the modern history of technological innovations in the process of making coins. The first coin in the Most Innovative category was the 1988 Albania 50 Leke, a large coin commemorating railroads. This large, impressive coin featured a piercing to represent part of a tunnel, a radical departure and advancement of coin design. A collection of these coins shows the evolution of minting technology and the willingness of world mints to experiment. They include coins on planchets that are not flat, like the 2001 France 1 Franc coin, and coins with non-metallic substances, like the 2009 British Indian Ocean Territory's 2 Pounds "Life of the Turtle."

A quick scan through the images in this book reveals the richness and diversity of medallic art spanning the last quarter century. In the early 1980s, Cliff Mishler and Chet Krause could not have anticipated that the dramatic embrace of modernism in medallic art that began at the end of WWII would become accepted as the norm on circulating world coin designs. The coins illustrated throughout this book are exceptional examples of the evolution of world coin design and provide a permanent record of the art of coins for this period.

Since ancient times, the artisans who created coins used in commerce were artists whose technique was ever evolving, carefully studied and appreciated as much as the monumental works in public squares and buildings. It is well known today that the most widely reproduced works of arts in the world are not housed in museums, but rather sit in the hands of commerce. Countless millions of Victor David Brenner's 1909 depiction of Abraham Lincoln have been appreciated and recognized around the world by countless millions of people. It is not "just a coin." It is a work of art.

The pages of this book present a contemporary history of the world and a history of contemporary art. Most of the coins remain available and affordable. A collection of coins in any one of the categories makes an attractive visual display, providing hours of fun and learning.

As a member of the U.S. Citizens Coinage Advisory Committee, I have hope that the many beautiful coin designs produced around the world will inspire American artists. Recent developments within the United States Mint are beginning to show a willingness to explore techniques like reverse proof, concave coins, and even higher relief. This is indeed an exciting time in numismatics and we owe a debt to Cliff Mishler, Chet Krause and all of the people who make the Krause Coin of the Year possible.

AWARDS

FOR COINS MINTED IN 1982

COIN OF THE YEAR

United States, 50-Cent, Silver,
250th Anniversary of the Birth of George Washington

It is fitting that the first coin selected as the Coin of the Year for the new award program was the first United States commemorative coin issued by the United States Mint since 1954. It won in both the Most Popular and the Most Historically Significant categories as well.

The coin theme selected to restart the United States commemorative coin program after a 28-year hiatus was the 250th anniversary of the birth of President George Washington. The task of designing the obverse and the reverse of this coin was assigned to Elizabeth Jones, Chief Sculptor and Engraver of the United States Mint.

The obverse bears the image of Washington on horseback wearing his uniform as General of the Continental Army. The image is cropped to allow Washington to appear prominently centered and seated erect as the curves in the horse flow with the curve of the coin and the horse's head occupies the right field to balance the word "Liberty" on the left.

The reverse depicts Mount Vernon, home of George and Martha Washington and the place where the President Washington was said to love more than any other place. Jones again uses the sloping landscape of Mount Vernon to create a slight curve at the bottom third of the design. The low angle creates the right perspective for one of the nicest depictions of buildings on coins ever created by a United States Mint artist.

Since the United States Mint had been out of the commemorative coin market for a long time and since the subject involved the most important man in the history of the United States, Congress authorized a maximum mintage of 10 million coins; 4,894,044 were actually minted. The Proof coins were manufactured at the San Francisco Mint and the uncirculated coins were made in Philadelphia.

While these coins are considered common, the Denver Mint State coins in MS69 are extremely rare and MS70 examples exist only in theory. The Proof coins, as usual with United States coins, are available and can be found in Proof-69 and Proof-70.

MOST HISTORICALLY SIGNIFICANT, MOST POPULAR

United States, 50-Cent, Silver, *250th Anniversary of the Birth of George Washington*

MOST ARTISTIC, BEST GOLD

Canada, 100-Dollar, Gold, *New Constitution 1982*

BEST SILVER
Panama, 20-Balboa, Silver,
*Balboa's Discovery of the
Pacific Ocean*

BEST CROWN
China, 20-Yuan,
Silver, *Year of the Dog*

1985

AWARDS

FOR COINS MINTED IN 1983

COIN OF THE YEAR

United States, 1 Dollar, Silver, Olympics Discus Thrower

The United States issued three coins to commemorate the Games of the XXIII Olympiad in Los Angeles, California. The first of the three coins, and only the second dollar denomination commemorative coin ever issued by the United States Mint, received the Coin of the Year Award for coins dated 1983. It also won the award for Most Popular Coin and Best Crown.

The discus throw lays claim to one of the events of the ancient pentathlon dating back to at least 700 B.C. The perfect form of the athlete coiled to make the throw is an image long associated with the Olympics. It was an appropriate choice to celebrate the 1984 Summer Olympics in Los Angeles, which also hosted the games in 1932.

The obverse design of a discus thrower was inspired by the ancient work of the sculptor Myron. Elizabeth Jones, the Chief Sculptor and Engraver of the United States Mint at the time, depicted the ancient art in a new and modern way by using a sculptural blur effect to show motion. The athlete is outlined twice and appears balanced toward the left of center with the Summer Olympic logo, also outlined twice on both sides in the right obverse field.

Jones depicts the bust of an eagle on the reverse. The eagle's head appears bold and proud against the inner ring containing the legend.

Congress optimistically authorized a maximum mintage of 50 Million coins for the three-coin set. Less than 1.2 million coins of all three coins in the set were sold. The 1983 silver dollar was by far the most popular of the three, accounting for more than half of the mintage of the set.

The uncirculated version of the 1983 Discus Thrower was minted in both Philadelphia and Denver. Proof versions were minted in San Francisco. None are particularly hard to find in high grades of MS69 or Proof-69.

MOST HISTORICALLY SIGNIFICANT
China, 5-Yuan, Silver,
Marco Polo

MOST POPULAR, BEST CROWN
United States, 1 Dollar, Silver,
Olympics Discus Thrower

MOST ARTISTIC
British Virgin Islands,
5-Dollar, Silver,
Yellow Warbler

BEST GOLD
(TIED)
Egypt, 100-Pound, Gold,
Cleopatra VII

BEST GOLD
(TIED)
China, 100-Yuan, Gold,
Panda

BEST SILVER
China, 10-Yuan, Silver,
Panda and Cub

1986

FOR COINS MINTED IN 1984

COIN OF THE YEAR

Canada, 100-Dollar, Gold,
450th Anniversary of Jacques Cartier Voyage of Discovery

The Canadian $100 gold commemorative coin honoring the 450th anniversary of Jacques Cartier's Voyage of Discovery won the Coin of the Year Award for coins dated 1984, becoming the first international winner. The judges also selected it as the winner in the Most Historically Significant coin. The impressive Canadian coin also tied with the Isle of Mann's first bullion gold coin for Best Gold Coin.

Canada's Cartier coin is part of a series of gold commemoratives. This one commemorates Jacques Cartier's landing at Gaspe Peninsula in Quebec. On April 20, 1534, Cartier set sail to "discover certain islands and lands where it is said that a great quantity of gold and other precious things are to be found." After some exploring in Newfoundland, he landed in Gaspe Bay and on July 24, 1534, he claimed the territory in the name of the King of France. This and his subsequent adventuress solidified the French claims to the St. Lawrence Seaway.

The Royal Canadian Mint held a competition to design this coin. Carola Tietz design was chosen over about 60 competitors. Unlike Elizabeth Jones at the United States Mint, Tietz had only designed two previous coins for the Canadian Mint. She designed the 1979 "Year of the Child" gold coin and a 1983 silver dollar commemorating the World University games in Edmonton. Walter Ott engraved the coin.

The obverse of the coin shows the portrait of Elizabeth II designed by A. Machin. The security lettering used on the edge of coins in 1983 was not continued in1984.

The Royal Canadian Mint displayed the coin at the opening of the Canada Pavilion during the 1984 Expo in Quebec and it was made available for sale to the public shortly thereafter. The Cartier commemorative 22kt gold coin exists only in proof. A total of 67,662 were minted so they are not terribly scarce in high grades up to MS69.

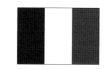

MOST HISTORICALLY SIGNIFICANT
France, 100-Franc, Gold,
*Two Time Nobel Prize Winner
Marie Curie*

**MOST HISTORICALLY SIGNIFICANT,
BEST GOLD**
Canada, 100-Dollar, Gold,
*450th Anniversary of Jacques
Cartier's Voyage of Discovery*

MOST POPULAR
United States, 1 Dollar, Silver,
*XXIII Olympic Games in Los,
Angeles, California*

**MOST ARTISTIC,
BEST SILVER**
Panama, 20-Balboa, Silver,
*Balboa Discovers the
Pacific Ocean*

BEST GOLD
Isle of Man, 1 Angel, Gold,
*Archangel Michael
Slaying the Dragon*

BEST CROWN
Barbados, 10-Dollar, Silver,
Three Dolphins

1987

AWARDS

FOR COINS MINTED IN 1985

COIN OF THE YEAR

Finland 50-Markkaa, Silver, Kalevala National Epic

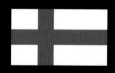

In addition to being named Coin of the Year, this remarkable offering from Finland won awards in three categories for coins dated 1985: Best Silver, Best Crown and Most Artistic.

Finland had broken the pictorial barrier on coin designs as early as the 1960s with coins like the 10-Markkaa honoring its 50th Anniversary of Independence (KM50) and other coins. However, the acknowledgement by the international community, including the still heavily weighted North American Coin of the Year jury panel, signaled an evolution in aesthetic preferences favoring a more abstract coin design.

The coin celebrates the 150th anniversary of the Kalevala, the Finnish national epic. This poem was part of the Finnish oral tradition for over 2,000 years. In 1835, Elias Lonnrot edited the poem and published it for the first time along with other epic poems in the Balto-Finnic language.

The obverse of the coin depicts trees reflected in the water of the Finnish countryside. The reverse depicts the hero of the epic poem standing amidst stylized waves.

Just as the publication of the Kalevala brought Finnish language and culture to the attention of the European community when it was published in 1835, this coin brought attention to Finnish medallic art and coin design to the world community for the first time in 1987.

Reijo Paavilainen and Tapio Nevalainen designed the coin. Paavilainen has been a member of The Guild of Medallic Art in Finland and has had the honor of designing several of their annual medals. His medallic art is a part of the permanent display at the Tampere Art Museum.

With its mintage of 300,000, this coin is relatively available, although grades above MS65 are scarce. The coin carries a privy mark, P-N, which probably stands for the designer and sculptor. No proof version was struck.

**MOST HISTORICALLY
SIGNIFICANT**
(TIED)
Austria, 500-Schilling,
Silver, *2000th Anniversary
of Bregenz*

**MOST HISTORICALLY
SIGNIFICANT**
(TIED)
India, 100-Rupee, Silver,
Indira Ghandi Memorial

MOST POPULAR
Canada, 20-Dollar, Silver,
*Olympics 1988
Downhill Skiing*

BEST GOLD
United Kingdom, 5-Pound,
Gold, *Saint George
Slaying the Dragon*

**BEST SILVER,
BEST CROWN**
Finland, 50-Markkaa, Silver,
Kalevala National Epic

BEST TRADE
Australia, 1 Dollar,
Copper-Aluminum-Nickel,
Kangaroos

AWARDS

FOR COINS MINTED IN 1986

COIN OF THE YEAR

United States, Five-Dollar, Gold, *Centennial of the Statue of Liberty*

The United States Congress authorized the first $5 gold coin since 1929 to honor the 100th Anniversary of the gift from France of the Statute of Liberty. It won the award for Most Popular Coin and became an obvious choice for Coin of the Year for coins dated 1986.

This was the third time in five years that the United States Mint took top honors. It was also the third time the Coin of the Year was awarded to a coin designed by Elizabeth Jones. The only woman to serve as Chief Engraver at the United States Mint, Jones is the only designer to receive the highest honor for her work three times. Jones served the U.S. Mint with distinction from 1981 to 1990.

For the United States, this would be the last Coin of the Year award until 2002. Criticism of the program having a North American prejudice was growing by 1988, something award founder Chester "Chet" Krause was aware of and feared would damage the goal of the program. Mr. Krause took steps to re-organize the judging process and in doing so secured the status of the Coin of the Year award as a truly international award of honor.

Both the proof and mint state versions of the gold coin were minted at the West Point Mint and bear the "W" mint mark. These were the first gold coins produced at West Point which would later be used to strike the American Gold Eagle coin series and other precious metal United States coins.

These coins were sold individually and as sets. Like many of the early modern United States commemoratives, the mintage was high with 95,248 sold. They are reasonably available in high grades of MS69 and Proof-69.

MOST HISTORICALLY SIGNIFICANT
Austria, 500-Schilling, Silver, *500th Anniversary of the Striking of the First Thaler Coin*

MOST POPULAR
United States, 5-Dollar, Gold, *Bicentennial of the Statue of Liberty*

MOST ARTISTIC
Western Samoa, 25-Tala, Silver, *Voyage of Kon-Tiki*

BEST GOLD
Japan, 100,000-Yen, Gold,
60th Year of the Reign of
Emperor Hirohito

BEST SILVER AND
BEST CROWN
Canada, 1 Dollar, Silver,
Centennial of Vancouver

BEST TRADE
(TIED)
Japan, 500-Yen, Cupronickel,
60th Year of the Reign of
Emperor Hirohito

BEST TRADE
(TIED)
Greece, 50 Drachmes,
Aluminum-Bronze,
Homer

1989

AWARDS

FOR COINS MINTED IN 1987

COIN OF THE YEAR

United Kingdom, 100-Pound, Gold, *Britannia*

It was a memorable year for the British Royal Mint. The Mint's 100-Pound gold Britannia, minted in 1987, was named not only the Coin of the Year but also the Best Gold Coin and Most Artistic Coin. It was an auspicious beginning for the first year of the British Royal Mint's gold bullion program.

The figure of a seated Britannia first appeared on the coins of the Roman Emperors. It was not until Charles II that the image was resurrected and placed on the coins of Great Britain. After decimalization of English coins, the seated Britannia was chosen to appear on the 50 Pence.

When the decision was made to issue international bullion gold, the figure of Britannia was a logical choice of an easily identifiable national image. Philip Nathan's design of a standing Britannia was ultimately selected for the new gold bullion coins.

The image of Britannia had always been portrayed seated until 1901 when the standing figure was used on the British trade dollars. In 1902 the standing Britannia was used on the Florins of Edward VII. Nathan adopted the standing Britannia. His Britannia holds a shield and an olive branch in one hand and a trident in the other. The draped figure glides on the ocean waves. The flowing gown suggests the movement of the ocean waves while the helmet and majesty of the standing figure depict the pride and power of the island nation and its dominance in the world.

The Britannia gold bullion coins were issued in four denominations: 100-Pound one ounce; 50-Pound half ounce; 25-Pound ¼ ounce; and the 10-Pound 1/10 ounce. All coins were issued in proof with a limited mintage and in uncirculated bullion with unlimited mintages. 13,000 proof one-ounce coins were minted.

**MOST HISTORICALLY
SIGNIFICANT**
United States, 5 Dollar, Gold,
*Bicentennial of the United
States' Constitution*

MOST POPULAR
United States, 1 Dollar,
Silver, *Bicentennial of the
United States' Constitution*

**MOST ARTISTIC,
BEST GOLD**
United Kingdom,
100-Pound, Gold, *Britannia*

BEST SILVER
Canada, 1 Dollar, Silver,
*400th Anniversary of the
Davis Straight*

BEST CROWN
Cook Islands, 50-Dollar,
Silver, *Seoul Olympic Games*

BEST TRADE
Switzerland, 5-Franc,
Cupronickel, *Centennial
of Le Corbusier*

AWARDS

FOR COINS MINTED IN 1988

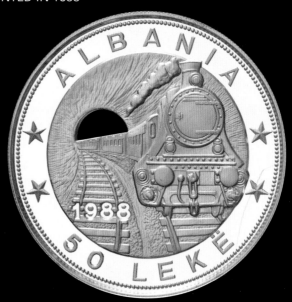

COIN OF THE YEAR

Albania, 50-Leke, Silver, *Railroads*

A new category called Most Innovative Coin Concept was introduced in 1990. As one of the first modern coins with a piercing, the Albania 50-Leke, Railroads, was an obvious winner in that category and it went on to gain support as the Coin of the Year.

This five-ounce silver coin minted in 1988 was the first oversized coin to win the award. The coin's diameter is 65 mm. The piercing is part of the design element that helps add a fourth dimension—time—to an otherwise three dimensional object. The train appears to come through the piercing which is the tunnel.

The obverse shows a steam locomotive and passenger train emerging from a tunnel. The reverse shows the train exiting the tunnel. Flipping the coin from obverse to reverse creates the illusion of the passage of time. This technique had been used previously in medallic art, however this is the first time the technique had been used effectively on a coin.

The coin was issued to commemorate the 42nd anniversary of Albanian railroads but in the broader sense commemorated the importance of rail in Albania. It was issued in proof only. However, the same design without the piercing was issued as a 5-Leke 38.7 copper-nickel coin, KM#61 for circulation. No proof of the smaller coin was made.

While the 50-Leke brings a premium over its silver content and is not often seen on the market, 7,500 were minted. While it is not a particularly rare coin, its absence from dealer trays is a testament to its popularity.

MOST HISTORICALLY SIGNIFICANT
Hungary, 500-Forint, Silver,
*950th Anniversary
of Saint Stephen*

MOST POPULAR
United States,
1 Dollar, Silver,
*Olympics 1988 Rings
and Wreath*

MOST ARTISTIC
Switzerland, 5-Franc,
Cupronickel,
Olympics Dove and Rings

MOST INNOVATIVE
Albania, 50-Leke, Silver,
Railroads

BEST GOLD
Egypt, 100-Pound, Gold,
Golden Warrior

BEST SILVER
China, 100-Yuan, Silver,
Year of the Dragon

BEST CROWN
Hungary, 500-Forint, Silver,
*25th Anniversary of the World
Wildlife Fund*

BEST TRADE
Australia, 50-Cent,
Cupronickel, *Bicentennial
of Australia*

1991

AWARDS

FOR COINS MINTED IN 1989

COIN OF THE YEAR

France, 5-Franc, Cupronickel, *Eiffel Tower*

The symbol of Paris and of France, the Eiffel Tower is one of the best-known monuments in the world. It is no surprise then that the coin commemorating the Tower's centennial would be the darling of the 1991 Awards. The French entry won honors as Best Trade, Most Popular and Most Artistic coin on its way to being named Coin of the Year.

Once described as "a vision, an object, a symbol, the Tower is anything that Man wants it to be, and this in infinite," work on the Eiffel Tower began in 1887. Gustave Eiffel built the tower for the 1889 Exposition Universelle, which was to celebrate the 100th anniversary of the French Revolution. Its construction was a technical and architectural achievement, a symbol of technological prowess at the end of the 19th century.

In addition to this coin, a painting reflecting its 100-year history commemorated the Eiffel Tower in 1989. The painting was unveiled in a location near the tower. The coin's obverse, designed by F. Joubert, features a unique perspective of the Eiffel tower as if taken with a wide-angle lens from beneath a supporting beam. The curve of the beam and the slant of the tower are rounded by the perspective to fill the planchet. The lettering on the right balances the image.

The reverse was designed by J. Jimenez and shows the tower from the bottom looking up. The denomination is stamped on the bottom of the inverted tower at the top half of the coin to provide balance to the image of the tower on the bottom half.

This is the first coin to receive the award that was struck in different alloys, but the copper nickel coin is the one the judges considered. The following metal varieties are available:

- KM968 Copper Nickel (Unc) 9,774,000 minted
- KM968a Silver (proof) 80,000 minted
- KM968b gold (proof) 30,000 minted

- KM968c platinum (proof) 1200 exist
- Piefort in platinum with only 10 made
- Essais in nickel in unknown quantity

While the platinum and the piefort versions are scarce, the copper nickel variety appears with some frequency.

**MOST HISTORICALLY
SIGNIFICANT,
MOST ARTISTIC**
United Kingdom, 1
Sovereign, Gold, *500th
Anniversary of the Gold
Sovereign*

MOST ARTISTIC
Israel, 2-New Sheqalim,
Silver, *41st Anniversary
of Israel*

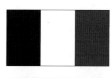

**MOST POPULAR,
MOST ARTISTIC,
BEST TRADE,**
France, 5-Franc,
Cupronickel, *Eiffel Tower*

BEST GOLD
Austria, 2,000-Schilling,
Gold, *Vienna Philharmonic
Orchestra*

BEST SILVER
Australia, 1 Dollar, Silver,
Holey Dollar

25-Cent, Silver,
*The Dump, Wandjina of
Aboriginal Mythology*

BEST CROWN
Spain, 5,000 Peseta, Silver,
*500th Anniversary of the
Discovery of America*

1992

— AWARDS —

FOR COINS MINTED IN 1990

COIN OF THE YEAR

Isle of Mann, 1 Crown, Cupronickel, *Penny Black*

One of the first coins to commemorate a stamp and to feature a stamp as its main design element won the Coin of the Year Award for coins dated 1990. This unique coin also won Best Crown and Most Innovative coin concept in the competition.

This Pobjoy Mint item commemorated the 150th anniversary of the world's first adhesive postage stamp. Known to stamp collectors as the "Penny Black," this stamp was the cornerstone to the reform of the British postal system. The stamp design is widely known in the stamp collecting community to all collectors and is based on a graphic design by famed engraver William Wyon.

One might say that the "Penny Black" was the forerunner of modern stamps. Prior to its issuance postage was paid on the delivery of a letter. Some marking was made on the envelope to indicate the price. Shortly after this stamp was issued, the adhesive postage stamp was adopted by country after country and became the standard everywhere in as little as two decades. The adhesive stamp is still used around the world.

This coin was minted in different alloys and in both proof and mint state. It came in various packaging options as well because the coin had an obvious appeal to the collector community reaching into the philatelic community. The copper nickel coin was the one considered by the Krause judges. A list of the other coin options:

- KM 267 Copper Nickel unc
- KM 267 Copper Nickel Proof 50,000 minted
- KM 267a Silver Proof 30,000 minted
- KM 267b Gold Proof 1,000 minted
- KM 267c Platinum Proof 50 minted

MOST HISTORICALLY SIGNIFICANT
Germany, 20-Mark, Cupronickel, *Opening of the Brandenburg Gate*

MOST POPULAR
Isle of Man, 1 Crown, Cupronickel, *Alley Cat*

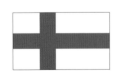

MOST ARTISTIC
Finland, 100-Markka, Silver, *50th Anniversary of Veterens*

**MOST INNOVATIVE,
BEST CROWN**
Isle of Man, 1 Crown,
Cupronickel, *Penny Black*

BEST GOLD
Russia, 25-Rouble,
Palladium, *Peter the Great*

BEST SILVER
France, 100-Franc, Silver,
Charlemagne

BEST TRADE
Denmark, 5-Kroner,
Cupronickel, *Queen
Margrethe II Monogram*

AWARDS

FOR COINS MINTED IN 1991

COIN OF THE YEAR

Italy, 500-Lire, Silver, *2100th Anniversary of the Ponte Milvio Bridge*

The coin dated 1991 that was voted Most Artistic Coin was also voted Krause Coin of the Year for that year. It commemorates the 2100th Anniversary of the Ponte Milvio Bridge.

Gaius Claudius Nero built the Ponte Milvio when he was consul of Rome in 206 BC as a commemoration of his defeat of the Carthaginians. The bridge was rebuilt many times since and it stands today as a critical commuter bridge in Rome.

While the Ponte Milvio is best known as the site of the famous battle between Constantine I and Maxentius in 312 that consolidated the rule of Constantine, who founded Constantinople, the capital of what became the Byzantine Empire, and who is best known for making Christianity the official religion of the Roman Empire.

Eugenio Drutti designed the winning coin. While the reverse is a fairly straightforward picture of the bridge, the obverse blends the ancient with the modern in an interesting way. The bridge and the ancient "SPQR" (The Senate and People of Rome) blend into the head of a young person as if to imply that the great history of Rome is a part of the mind of every modern Italian.

The coin was minted in proof and in mint state and made available through special sets. The Mint state version was placed in a capsule at the mint so it usually comes in MS65 or better. 59,000 coins were made and they are reasonably available in the market.

MOST HISTORICALLY SIGNIFICANT
Russia, 3-Rouble, Silver, *Yuri Gagarin First Man in Space*

MOST POPULAR
Australia, 5-Dollar, Silver, *Kookaburra*

MOST ARTISTIC
Italy, 500-Lire, Silver, *2,100th Anniversary of Ponte Milvio Bridge*

BEST GOLD
Japan, 100,000- Yen, Gold, *Enthronement of the Emperor*

**MOST INNOVATIVE,
BEST SILVER**
Albania, 10-Leke, Silver,
Olympics Equestrian

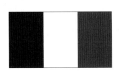

BEST CROWN
France, 100-Franc, Silver,
Olympics Ski Jump

BEST TRADE
Portugal, 200-Escudo,
Aluminum-Bronze-
Cupronickel, *Garcia De Orta*

AWARDS

FOR COINS MINTED IN 1992

COIN OF THE YEAR

Italy, 500-Lire, Silver, *Flora and Fauna*

When judges voted the 500-Lire entry from Italy as the Coin of the Year, as well as Most Artistic Coin, it marked the first time that a county other than the United States won the competition two years in a row.

As of 2002 there were more than 400 species of mammals and birds and about 6,000 species of plants throughout Italy. Italy honored its plant and animal life by adding it to their commemorative coin series of 500-Lire silver coins.

The Italian countryside varies in elevation and climate, creating a home for a diverse plant and animal life. Flora is found above 7,500 feet in the Apennines and oak trees, chestnut trees, beach trees and conifers grow on the slopes. Mediterranean vegetation predominates on the bulk of the peninsula. Plant life along with a bird and some butterflies adorn the coin's obverse juxtaposed against the head of woman.

The animal life is also varied. Bears and roe deer inhabit the Apennines and the Alps, while varied animal life inhabit the peninsula. The reverse of the coin shows a fish, a bird and a reptile indigenous to Italy but located at different elevations. Carmela Colaneri designed the coin using the square as if to portray a window to view the images on the obverse and reverse.

The mint state coins were sold in a folder describing the plant and animal life of Italy; 43,000 were sold. The proof coins were sold encapsulated and placed in a box with a descriptive leaflet; 6,300 were sold. Both of these coins are relatively available.

MOST HISTORICALLY SIGNIFICANT
Russia, 1 Ruble, Cupronickel,
Rebirth of Sovereignty

MOST POPULAR
United States, 1 Dollar,
Silver, *White House*

MOST ARTISTIC
Italy, 500-Lire, Silver,
Flora and Fauna

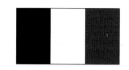

MOST INNOVATIVE, BEST TRADE
France, 20-Franc,
Tri-Metallic,
Mont Saint Michel

BEST GOLD
United States, 5-Dollar, Gold,
Christopher Columbus

BEST SILVER
Spain, 2,000 Peseta, Silver,
Barcelona Olympics

BEST CROWN
Austria, 100-Schilling, Silver,
Kaiser Karl V

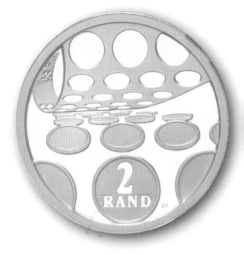

**SPECIAL
RECOGNITION
FOR MERIT OF DESIGN**
South Africa, 2-Rand, Silver,
Minting Process

AWARDS

FOR COINS MINTED IN 1993

COIN OF THE YEAR

France, 500 Franc, Gold, *Louvre Museum—Mona Lisa*

The 500 Franc gold Bicentennial of the Louvre with the reproduction of Leonardo da Vinci's *Mona Lisa* on the obverse won the Best Gold Coin award as well as the Coin of the Year Award for coins dated 1993. France also won the Most Historically Significant Coin honor with its 1 Franc silver D-Day commemorative.

The *Mona Lisa* was part of a gold and silver miniseries celebrating the bicentennial of the Louvre. It was issued in both proof and mint state both in 1993 and again in 1994 as a proof-only issue. The other coins in the set reproduce the images of the *Venus de Milo*, the Delacroix's *Liberty Guiding the People*, the *Samothrace Victory*, the *Marie-Marquerite* and the painting of *Napoleon Crowning Josephine as Empress*. Five-ounce gold proof-only coins of these designs were issued in 1993 and 1994 with a mintage of less than 100.

All of the coins in both the 100 Franc and 500 Franc denomination share a common reverse showing the facade of the Louvre along with Pei's glass pyramid standing in front of it. The Louvre is the world's largest museum and houses one of the most impressive art collections in history. The magnificent, baroque-style palace and museum — LeMusée du Louvre in French — sits along the banks of the Seine River in Paris. These coins were issued to commemorate the rich history of the museum since it was founded.

The gold coins were issued in both one ounce and five ounces carrying a denomination of 500 Francs. The one-ounce coins have a mintage of about 5,000 and the five-ounce coins have a mintage of less than 100. While the five-ounce coins rarely appear for sale, the silver 100 Franc coins are often seen in sets of six. The one-ounce gold 500 Franc coins, while not rare, appear infrequently as do their 100 Franc gold siblings.

**MOST HISTORICALLY
SIGNIFICANT**
France, 1 Franc, Silver,
D-Day

MOST POPULAR
Gibraltar, 1 Crown,
Cupronickel,
Stegosaurus

MOST ARTISTIC
Austria, 500 Schillings,
Silver, *Halstatt*

MOST INNOVATIVE
Andorra, 20-Diner European
Currency Unit, Silver,
Saint George

MOST INSPIRATIONAL
Poland, 300,000-Zlotych,
Silver, *Warsaw Ghetto
Uprising*

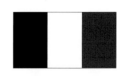

BEST GOLD
France, 500 Francs, Gold,
Louvre Museum, Mona Lisa

BEST SILVER
China, 150 Yuan, Silver,
Peacocks

BEST CROWN
Fiji, 10 Dollars, Silver,
Captain William Bligh

BEST TRADE
Czech Republic, 50 Korun,
Bi-Metallic, *Prague City*

AWARDS

FOR COINS MINTED IN 1994

COIN OF THE YEAR

United Kingdom, 50 Pence, Cupronickel,
50th Anniversary of the Invasion of Normandy

The celebration of the 50th anniversary of the invasion of Normandy was the subject of the United Kingdom's 50 Pence copper-nickel coin. It won Best Contemporary Event and Most Popular honors, as well as walking away with the top prize of Coin of the Year for coins dated 1994. As stated in the leaflet that accompanies the coin:

It was realized that an invasion was likely in the summer of 1944 but the exact date and location remained one of the best kept secrets of the War. Thus Operation Overlord, one of the most difficult military operations ever undertaken, was able to begin just after midnight on 6 June, 1944—in the first hour of the day that would forever be known as D-Day.

The allied invasion force filling the sea and sky and heading for Normandy on 6 June 1944 is vividly captured on this splendid commemorative coin. The design was created by award winning sculptor John Mills and was inspired by his boyhood recollections of that historic day. Looking up at the sky he saw it filled with distinctively marked planes and realized that the invasion of France was underway.

John Mills is a past president of the Royal British Society of Sculptors and his monumental work appears throughout London. His more well known pieces include the National Firefighters Memorial in front of St. Paul's Cathedral and the Monument to the Women of World War II near Whitehall.

While the committee considers the copper-nickel version of the coin as the award winner, the British Royal Mint issued this coin in a variety of options and offered as a single and in sets:
- KM#966 Copper Nickel in proof and mint state
- KM#966a, silver proof

**MOST HISTORICALLY
SIGNIFICANT**
United States, 1 Dollar, Silver,
*Thomas Jefferson
Architect of Democracy*

**MOST POPULAR,
BEST
CONTEMPORARY
EVENT**
United Kingdom,
50 Pence, Cupronickel,
*50th Anniversary of the
Invasion of Normandy*

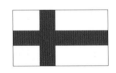

MOST ARTISTIC
Finland, 100 Markkaa, Silver,
*European Athletic
Championships*

MOST INNOVATIVE
Bahamas, 5 Dollars, Silver,
Golf, Hole In One

MOST INSPIRATIONAL
Poland, 300,000 Zlotych,
Silver, *Warsaw Uprising*

BEST GOLD
Austria, 1,000 Schillings,
Gold/Silver,
*800th Anniversary of
the Vienna Mint*

BEST SILVER
Italy, 1,000 Lire, *Silver,*
400th Anniversary
of Tintoretto

BEST CROWN
France, 100 Francs, Silver,
Olympics, Javelin Thrower

BEST TRADE
France, 20 Franc,
Tri-Metallic,
Pierre de Coubertin

1997

— AWARDS —

FOR COINS MINTED IN 1995

COIN OF THE YEAR

Finland, 100 Markkaa, Silver, *50th Anniversary of the United Nations*

Celebrating the 50th anniversary of the United Nations, Finland won Coin of the Year with a design by Reijo Paavilainen. The entry also won Best Silver Coin and Most Artistic Coin honors in the competition.

Several countries commemorated the 50th anniversary of the United Nations with coins. As it was, Finland issued two coins for this anniversary: a gold 2000 Markkaa and the silver 100 Markkaa. For Finland, the anniversary of the United Nations coincided with joining the European Union.

Paavilainen's design depicts a stylized dove with olive branch on the obverse. Both the obverse and the reverse of the coin use straight lines with part of the central image breaking through. On the obverse, the dove's wings are stylized to cut a line between the relief and the field. On the reverse, two straight lines forming a triangle against the edge of the coin separate the relief from the field. The curved branch breaks the line.

This coin exists in proof with a mintage of 3,000 and in uncirculated with a mintage of 40,000. The uncirculated version is relatively common and the proof comes up from time to time. Grades up to MS67 and Proof-68 can be expected. Higher grades are rare.

MOST HISTORICALLY SIGNIFICANT

Germany, 10 Marks, Silver,
Centennial of the X-ray

MOST POPULAR

United States,
50 Cents, Silver,
Olympic Baseball

MOST ARTISTIC, BEST SILVER

Finland, 100 Markkaa, Silver,
50th Anniversary of the United Nations

MOST INNOVATIVE
Austria, 500 Schilling,
Bi-Metallic,
*Austria in the
European Union*

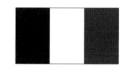

**MOST INSPIRATIONAL,
BEST GOLD**
France, 500 Franc, Gold,
*50th Anniversary of
Victory in Europe (V.E.) Day*

BEST CROWN
Austria, 200 Schilling, Silver,
Olympics, Ribbon Dancer

BEST TRADE
Australia, 1 Dollar,
Aluminum, Bronze,
Waltzing Matilda

**BEST
CONTEMPORARY
EVENT**
Russia, 100 Rouble, Silver,
*50th Anniversary of the
End of World War II*

1998

AWARDS

FOR COINS MINTED IN 1996

COIN OF THE YEAR

Bermuda, 60 Dollars, Gold, *Bermuda Triangle*

Bermuda's first coin in the shape of a triangle, the Bermuda 60 Dollar gold coin depicting the Bermuda Triangle on the reverse, was selected as the Most Innovative Coin for design and received the Coin of the Year Award for coins dated 1996.

Known for centuries as the "Isle of Devils" because of the hazardous reefs, bad storms and tropical wildlife that makes uncommon sounds, Bermuda gave rise to a legend that its location causes mysterious disappearances. The first coin in a three-coin series honoring Bermuda's maritime tradition depicts the islands of Bermuda. The coin was marketed and titled "Bermuda Triangle" because of the triangular planchet shape.

Robert Elderton's design for the reverse of the coin depicts the discovery and mapping of the islands of Bermuda. The island chain is depicted in the style of a map. It is positioned between a compass rose and a sixteenth century Spanish Caravel in full sail. The Caravel was the style of ship that Christopher Columbus and the early Spanish explorers sailed when they originally discovered and charted the islands. A single rope with an overhand knot in each corner is used as a border separating the design from the legend on each side.

Although these coins are legal tender in Bermuda they were struck only in proof for collectors. While judges selected the 60 Dollar gold coin as the nominee, there are four denominations. The 30 Dollar gold coin is the most difficult to find. Nice examples of the 5-ounce 9 Dollar coin are also somewhat scarce.

- KM#92, 1996 Proof $3 silver ½ ounce (about 5,000 minted)
- KM#96, 1996 Proof $9 silver 5 ounce (about 1,000 minted)
- KM#97, 1996 Proof $30 gold ½ ounce (less than 1,000 minted)
- KM#93, 1996 Proof $60 gold 1 ounce (about 1500 minted)

**MOST HISTORICALLY
SIGNIFICANT**
Israel, 30 New Sheqalim,
Silver, *3,000th Anniversary
of Jerusalem*

**MOST POPULAR,
BEST TRADE**
Canada, 2 Dollar,
Bi-Metallic,
Polar Bear

MOST ARTISTIC
Finland, 100 Markkaa, Silver,
Helene Schjerfbeck

**MOST INNOVATIVE,
BEST GOLD**
Bermuda, 60 Dollars, Gold,
Bermuda Triangle

MOST INSPIRATIONAL
United States, 1 Dollar,
Silver, *Paralympics*

BEST SILVER
Russia, 100 Rouble, Silver,
*The Nutcracker Ballet,
Marsha and the Nutcracker*

BEST CROWN
Austria, 500 Schillings, Silver, *Innsbruck Town Market*

BEST CONTEMPORARY EVENT
Bosnia-Herzegovina, 14 Euro, Silver, *Dayton Peace Accord*

1999

AWARDS

FOR COINS MINTED IN 1997

COIN OF THE YEAR

South Africa, 1 Rand, Silver, *Women of South Africa*

South Africa won several awards for coins dated 1997. The 1 Rand gold, *First Heart Transplant* commemorative, won the award for Best Contemporary Event. The 1 Rand silver, *Women of South Africa*, won the Most Artistic Coin and went on to win the Coin of the Year.

By 1997, the plight of women in South Africa had been recognized by various human rights groups around the world. Writing on the subject, Waheeda Amien, Gender Convener at the legal aid clinic for the University of South Africa said, "Although women comprise 52% of the South African population, it has been acknowledged that they constitute one of the most marginalized and vulnerable groups in this country."

The obverse design by A.L. Sutherland depicts the king protea, the national flower of South Africa, in full bloom. It is set in the center of the coin with clean fields on either side. The country name and date is above and below respectively. This design has since been used as the obverse of other 1 Rand coins of South Africa.

Susan Erasmus' reverse design is an interesting frontal view of a woman's face cracked by the South African countryside. Below is a lunar landscape. The earth and the moon blend together in the design. They form the coins relief along with the woman's face suggesting mother earth flowing into sister moon. The word, "protea" creates a link to the flower on the reverse and identifies the coin's South African focus.

As most coins of South Africa, this one is rare in any grade. In uncirculated, 3,312 were minted and 2,329 were minted in proof.

**MOST HISTORICALLY
SIGNIFICANT**
Canada, 100 Dollars, Gold,
Alexander Graham Bell

MOST POPULAR
United States,
100 Dollars, Platinum,
Statue of Liberty, Eagle

MOST ARTISTIC
South Africa, 1 Rand, Silver,
Women of South Africa

MOST INNOVATIVE
Kiribati & Western Samoa,
5 Dollars, Silver,
War and Peace

MOST INSPIRATIONAL
Sierra Leon, 10 Leon, Silver,
*Mother Teresa and
Princess Diana*

BEST GOLD
Canada, 200 Dollars, Gold,
Haida Carved Mask

BEST SILVER

Austria, 100 Schillings, Silver,
Emperor Maximilian
of Mexico

BEST CROWN

United Kingdom, 2 Pounds,
Silver, *Britannia*

BEST TRADE

Poland, 2 Zlote, Brass,
Pieskowa Skala Castle

**BEST
CONTEMPORARY
EVENT**

South Africa, 1 Rand, Gold,
First Heart Transplant

2000

AWARDS

FOR COINS MINTED IN 1998

COIN OF THE YEAR

Austria, 500 Schillings, Silver, *Book Printing*

Austria won the Coin of the Year honor, as well as Best Silver Coin, for its 500 Schilling silver coin dated 1998 commemorating book printing. Austria also won the Best Trade Coin award for its 50 Schilling bi-metal celebrating the Austrian president of the European Union.

The reverse of the Coin of the Year designed by Thomas Pesendorfer shows an interior view of Adimont Abbey Library. Perhaps it was chosen because it houses the largest collection of manuscripts copied by medieval monks in the world. Located at the site of former Benedictine monastery, the main hall was built in 1776 and became the largest library in the world at the time.

The artist's choice to use the interior design of the main hall on the reverse brings together the history of printing by blending the collection of medieval manuscripts on the shelves with the enlightenment style of architecture. The floor space creates a field for the country name, denomination and date.

The obverse designed by Herbert Wahner shows printers at work. Austria has a claim to being the origin of movable type printing allowing books to be mass-produced in the early Renaissance. Arguably the world's most famous printer was German-born Johannes Gutenberg, who is credited with printing the world's first book using movable type and ushering in the age of mass communication.

Austria minted this coin for circulation as well as for collectors. The circulation strike with a mintage of 68,000 is most commonly found in grades below MS65. Higher grade uncirculated specimens most likely came from the special uncirculated strike made for collectors and sold in capsules from the Mint. 40,000 proof coins were minted and these typically come in high grades averaging Proof-67. They were sold in official mint boxes.

**MOST HISTORICALLY
SIGNIFICANT**

Portugal, 200 Escudos,
Cupronickel,
*500th Anniversary of the
Voyage to India*

MOST POPULAR

Canada, 1 Dollar, Silver,
*125th Anniversary of the
Royal Canadian Mounted
Police*

MOST ARTISTIC

Andorra, 10 Diners, Silver,
Europa Driving a Quadriga

MOST INNOVATIVE

Cook Islands, Fiji,
Western Samoa,
2 Dollars, Silver
*Three Coin Set, Tripartite
Convention*

MOST INSPIRATIONAL

Bosnia-Herzegovina,
14 Euro, Silver,
Dove of Peace

BEST GOLD

Singapore, 250 Dollar, Gold,
Year of the Tiger

BEST SILVER
Austria, 500 Schilling, Silver,
Book Printing

BEST CROWN
Portugal, 1,000 Escudos,
*Silver, International
Oceans Exposition*

BEST TRADE
Austria, 50 Schilling,
Bi-Metallic,
*Austrian Presidency of
the European Union*

BEST
CONTEMPORARY
EVENT
Israel,
2 New Sheqalim, Silver,
50th Anniversary of Israel

— AWARDS —

FOR COINS MINTED IN 1999

COIN OF THE YEAR

Italy, 5,000 Lira, Silver, *World Encircled by Birds and Stars*

While both the United Kingdom and the United States had two coins winning in categories this year, it was Italy's *World Encircled by Birds and Stars* coin for the new millennium that won the Coin of the Year. This was the third time Italy won the high prize.

Laura Cretara's obverse design depicts a globe with latitude and longitude markings. It is circled by an elliptical hallo of stars with three birds flying along its path. The ellipse separates the central design from the country name and date along the edge. The earth is in high relief.

The reverse depicts wheels and a satellite dish. The wheel is both a form of transportation and communication. The design depicts a wagon wheel, a ship's steering wheel and a concave satellite dish. The placement of the satellite dish in this image shows the evolution of the wheel in the last millennium. Three bands with stylized ground, ocean and stars complement the three wheels.

Italy used the obverse of this coin design again for the 10,000 Lira silver new millennium coin in 2000. It was paired with a new reverse that depicts Leonardo Da Vinci's wing and airplane design. Between 1999 and 2002 Italy was still using the Lira even though it had switched to the Euro.

This coin is not particularly hard to find and comes in grades averaging MS65 or Proof-67. There were 37,600 mint state coins minted and sold with an information card. There were 8170 proof coins made. They were also sold in sets with 5000 Lira Birds Sprouting from Globe design, KM#197, minted that year.

**MOST HISTORICALLY
SIGNIFICANT**
Austria, 100 Schilling, Silver,
*Assassination of Archduke
Franz Ferdinand*

MOST POPULAR
United Kingdom,
5 Pounds, Cupronickel,
Diana, Princess of Wales

MOST ARTISTIC
Italy, 5,000 Lire, Silver,
*World Encircled by
Birds and Stars*

MOST INNOVATIVE
Latvia, 1 Lats, Silver,
Millennium, Button

MOST INSPIRATIONAL
Ukraine, 10 Hyrven,
Silver, *Birth of Jesus*

BEST GOLD
Czech Republic,
10,000 Korun, Gold,
Charles IV

BEST SILVER
United Kingdom,
2 Pound, Silver,
Britannia in a Chariot

BEST CROWN
United States, 1 Dollar,
Silver, *Dolley Madison*

BEST TRADE
United States, 25 Cent, Clad,
*New Jersey, Crossroads
of the Revolution*

**BEST
CONTEMPORARY
EVENT**
Austria, 50 Schilling,
Bi-Metallic,
European Monetary Union

2002

AWARDS

FOR COINS MINTED IN 2000

COIN OF THE YEAR

United States, 1 Dollar, Silver, Voyage of Leif Ericson

The United States received the award for Most Historically Significant Coin and, for the first time since the 1986 *Centennial of the Statue of Liberty* gold $5 coin, the Coin of the Year for coins dated 2000.

John Mercanti designed the portrait of a helmeted Viking voyager. In the absence of any portraits of Leif Ericson, Mercanti conceived of a generic Nordic face with long hair protruding from the helmut, a beard and a bushy mustache and eyebrows. The portrait looks a lot like a crusty New England sailing captain, which might have been the Mercanti's intention.

T. James Ferrell designed the reverse design depicting a Viking ship under sail. The image is the best guess at the type of ship that Leif Ericson might have used around the time he landed on what was probably the northern tip of Newfoundland in 1000 A.D.

This is the first time the United States Mint worked collaboratively with a foreign mint to market a product. Iceland issued a 1000 Kroner silver coin honoring Leif Ericson the same year. Throstur Magnusson's design depicts his interpretation of the Stirling Calder statue of Leif Ericson on the obverse and a stylized drawing of the Icelandic Coat of Arms on the reverse. The Calder statue was a gift by the United States to the people of Iceland in 1930 to commemorate the millennium of the Iceland Parliament.

As all United States commemorative coins, this coin was authorized by the Congress of the United States as Public Law: 106-126 with high mintage limits of 500,000 which was not reached. This coin is easily obtainable in grades of MS68 and MS69, while grades of MS70 coins exist. The Proof coins in a Proof-70 grade are extremely rare, but it is not hard to find them in Proof-69. They were minted at the Philadelphia Mint and bear the "P" mintmark.

**MOST HISTORICALLY
SIGNIFICANT**
United States, 1 Dollar, Silver,
Voyage of Leif Ericson

MOST POPULAR
United States, 1 Dollar,
Copper, Zinc, Manganese,
Nickel, *Sacagawea*

MOST ARTISTIC
Lithuania, 50-Litu, Silver,
Discus Thrower

MOST INNOVATIVE
Japan, 500 Yen, Copper, *Zinc,
Nickel, Paulownia Flower*

MOST INSPIRATIONAL
Australia, 5 Dollars,
Aluminum, Bronze,
Paralympics

BEST GOLD
Canada, 200 Dollars, Gold,
Inuit Mother and Child

BEST SILVER
Mexico, 1 Onza, Silver,
Winged Victory

BEST CROWN
Austria, 100 Schilling,
Silver, *Celtic Heritage*

BEST TRADE
Australia, 50 Cents,
Cupronickel,
Visit by Queen Elizabeth II

BEST
CONTEMPORARY
EVENT
Germany, 10 Marks, Silver,
*10th Anniversary of
German Reunification*

2003

— AWARDS —

FOR COINS MINTED IN 2001

COIN OF THE YEAR

France 1 Franc, Silver, *The Last Franc*

The 2003 Coin of the Year awards proved a grand going away party for the Franc. France's salute to its national currency won both the Coin of the Year and Most Innovative Coin for coins dated 2001.

The name of the French currency unit 2001 was derived from the Latin inscription, "Francorum rex" that appeared on a gold coin of King John II in 1360. It became the national currency in 1795. When France switched to the Euro, the 1 Euro coin was valued at 6.5 Francs. The Franc was demonetized on February 28, 2002. This coin was issued just a few months earlier on September 1, 2001.

To commemorate the end of a long run of coins the Paris Mint worked with Philippe Starck to design a coin in the shape of a wave or discarded planchet found in the Mint's reject bin. The obverse bears a number "1" with the serif edges cut off by the rim. The reverse bears only the inscription, "un ultime franc" the "c" in franc only partly appearing. The date, country and motto are inscribed faintly on the rim.

Although this coin was never intended for circulation, it was a fitting tribute to the end of an era in French coinage. By 2001 more than 36 countries used the Franc as the denomination of their country's coinage.

Paris Mint officials were stunned by the success of this coin. 49,838 were minted. The coin was also issued in gold with a mintage of 4,963. Both the silver and gold coins are readily available in grades of MS66 to MS68.

MOST HISTORICALLY SIGNIFICANT
Australia, 10 Dollar, Silver,
The Evolution of the Calendar

MOST POPULAR
United States, 1 Dollar,
Silver, *Buffalo*

MOST ARTISTIC
Russia, 25 Rouble, Silver,
*225th Anniversary of
the Bolshoi Theater*

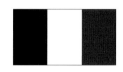

MOST INNOVATIVE
France, 1 Franc, Silver,
The Last Franc

MOST INSPIRATIONAL
Gibraltar, 1 Crown,
Cupronickel,
Florence Nightingale

BEST GOLD
China, 500 Yuan,
Gold, *Panda*

BEST SILVER
China, 20 Yuan, Silver,
Mogao Grottoes

BEST CROWN
Australia, 1 Dollar, Silver,
Aboriginal Kangaroo

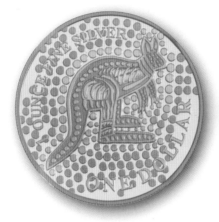

BEST TRADE
United States, 25 Cents, Clad,
Rhode Island, The Ocean State

**BEST
CONTEMPORARY
EVENT**
Belgium, 500 Franc,
Silver, *The Birth of
the European Euro*

2004

— AWARDS —

FOR COINS MINTED IN 2002

COIN OF THE YEAR

2002 Austria, 5 Euro, Silver, *Schoenbrunn Zoo*

Austria's 5 Euro coin, commemorating the 250th anniversary of the Schoenbrunn Zoo, earned both the Coin of the Year and Most Popular Coin for coins dated 2002.

The Schoenbrunn Zoo is the oldest continuously operated zoo in the world. It was founded by Empress Maria Theresa and her husband Franz Stephan Von Lothringen in a park in Schoenbrunn and originally consisted of 12 animal enclosures, a pond and two farmyards. After the central pavilion and the wall were erected, animals were brought to the zoo and it opened to the public in the summer of 1752.

Helmut Andexlinger's reverse design shows the pavilion surrounded by some of the zoo animals. The pavilion is in the center of the coin with the commemorative inscription above and the anniversary dates below.

The nine points of the coin symbolize the nine federal provinces of Austria. Herbert Wahner uses these nine points of his sun with rays design. The connection between the coin's design and shape adds power to the symbolism of unity, history and enlightenment. The coats of arms of each of the nine provinces between the slopes of the star points encircle the denomination. Wahner's obverse design on a nine-sided planchet has been used as the standard obverse on 5 Euro commemorative coins ever since.

These coins were sold in capsules and in a blister pack with a description of the coin with a mintage of 100,000. More were sold at the gift shop in the zoo. These were offered in four different packages, each showing a different zoo animal. 500,000 were struck making this coin quite common.

**MOST HISTORICALLY
SIGNIFICANT**
United States, 25 Cent, Clad,
*Ohio, Birthplace of
Aviation Pioneers*

MOST POPULAR
Austria, 5 Euro, Silver,
Schoenbrunn Zoo

MOST ARTISTIC
Latvia, 1 Lats, Silver,
Destiny, Roots

MOST INNOVATIVE
Isle of Man,
60 Pence, Bronze, Silver,
Currency Converter

MOST INSPIRATIONAL
Alderney, 5 Pound, Silver,
Princess Diana of Wales

BEST GOLD
Austria, 50 Euro, Gold,
*The Order of Saint Benedict
and the Order of Saint
Scholastica*

BEST SILVER
Austria, 10 Euro, Silver,
Ambras Palace

BEST CROWN
United States,
1 Dollar, Silver,
West Point Military Academy

BEST TRADE
Brazil, 1 Real,
Bi-Metallic, *Liberty*

**BEST
CONTEMPORARY
EVENT**
United Kingdom,
5 Pound, Gold,
*50th Anniversary of the Reign
of Queen Elizabeth II*

AWARDS

FOR COINS MINTED IN 2003

COIN OF THE YEAR

Belarus, 100 Rouble, Silver, *Belarus Ballet*

Belarus took the award for Best Crown Coin with its 20 Rouble, *Mute Swan*, and for Most Artistic Coin with the 100 Rouble, Belarus Ballet. The 100 Rouble earned Coin of the Year for coins dated 2003. It was the second time that a five-ounce silver coin won top honors.

Svetlana Zaskevich, an artist at the National Bank of Belarus, designed this coin and it was minted at the Lithuanian Mint for the Republic of Belarus.

The obverse depicts the National Academic Bolshoi Opera and Ballet Theater of the Republic of Belarus. Above it is the state coat of arms with the inscription, "Republic of Belarus." The face value of the coin is written in script at the bottom of the obverse under the year.

The reverse is a scene from the national ballet, *Passions*, by Andrey Mdivani and the inscription in two lines, "Ballet Belarusian." Two dancers glide across the proof surface of the coin reaching the edge as if to fall gracefully off the coin's surface. The dancers embrace and look into each other's eyes with delicate facial expressions.

Unlike many of the 100 Rouble five-ounce coins of Belarus, no 20 Rouble equivalent of this coin exists. With the low proof mintage of 1,000, this is one of the rarest coins to receive the Coin of the Year award. As a result of the demand for this coin after it received the Award, the reverse design was used again beginning in 2006 for other gold coins of Belarus in denominations of 10, 200 and 1000 Roubles.

MOST HISTORICALLY SIGNIFICANT
Australia, 10 Dollar, Silver,
Evolution of the Alphabet

MOST POPULAR
New Zealand, 1 Dollar,
Nickel, *Brass,*
The Lord of the Rings

MOST ARTISTIC
Belarus, 100 Rouble,
Silver, *Belarus Ballet*

MOST INNOVATIVE
Cook Islands, 1 Dollar, Silver,
*Emerald, Gemstone
Zodiac Locket*

MOST INSPIRATIONAL
Australia, 50 Cents,
Cupronickel,
Australia's Volunteers

BEST GOLD
Austria, 100 Euro, Gold,
Klimt's "The Kiss"

BEST SILVER
Spain, 10 Euro, Silver,
*75th Anniversary of
the School Ship, El Cano*

BEST CROWN
Belarus, 20-Rouble,
Silver, *Mute Swan*

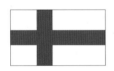

BEST TRADE
Finland, 5 Euro, Bi-metallic,
*Ice Hockey World
Championships*

BEST
CONTEMPORARY
EVENT
United Kingdom,
2 Pound, Bi-Metallic,
The Discovery of DNA

AWARDS

FOR COINS MINTED IN 2004

COIN OF THE YEAR
Italy, 5 Euro, Silver, *Madame Butterfly*

Italy won the Coin of the Year Award for the fourth time in 2006. The 5 Euro *Madame Butterfly* won the award for Most Artistic Coin and then went on to win the top honor for coins dated 2004.

Italy celebrated the 100th anniversary of the first performance of Giacomo Puccini's opera, "Madame Butterfly," by issuing two coins, a 5 Euro and a 10 Euro. In earning the top honor for the fourth time, Italy tied the United States for winning the most Coin of the Year awards.

Luciana de Simoni designed the coin. The obverse of the 5 Euro coin depicts the La Scala opera house in Milan where "Madame Butterfly" was initially performed in 1904. An encircled bird is perched on a branch above the opera house unifying the obverse and reverse with the attached foliage.

The reverse depicts an image of Madame Butterfly while waiting in her home in Japan for her American husband to return. This image, which may have been taken from the statue next to the statue of Puccini in Milan, or it may be the artist's representation of Rosina Storchio, the fist soprano to play the part of Madame Butterfly in 1904.

These coins were sold in a set with the 10 Euro Puccini coin in both proof and uncirculated with 12,000 proof coins minted. They were sold singly and in sets with the 10 Euro of Giacomo Puccini. 30,000 mint state coins were made. Proof and uncirculated specimens are not difficult to find.

MOST HISTORICALLY SIGNIFICANT

United States, 1 Dollar, Silver, *125th Anniversary of Edison's Electric Light*

MOST POPULAR

France, 1.5 Euro, Silver, *FIFA Soccer*

MOST ARTISTIC

Italy, 5 Euro, Silver, *Madame Butterfly*

MOST INNOVATIVE
Liberia, 10 Dollar, Silver,
*Window with
Tiffany Glass Inlay*

MOST INSPIRATIONAL
Poland, 20 Zlotych, Silver,
Victims of the Lodz Ghetto

BEST GOLD
China, 2,000 Yuan, *Gold,
Maijishan Grottoes*

BEST SILVER
Australia, 1 Dollar, Silver,
Kangaroo

BEST CROWN
Cyprus, 1 Pound,
Cupronickle,
Triton Sounding a Conch

BEST TRADE
Greece, 2 Euro, Bi-Metallic,
Olympic Discus Thrower

BEST CONTEMPORARY EVENT
Alderney, 50 Pound, Silver,
*60th Anniversary of D-Day
Invasion of Normandy*

AWARDS

FOR COINS MINTED IN 2005

COIN OF THE YEAR

United States, 1 Dollar, Silver, *U.S. Marine Corps*

The United States Silver 1 Dollar salute to the Marine Corps won the Best Crown for coins dated 2005. It marched off with the Coin of the Year award as well, marking the fifth time the United States won high honors and in the process surpassing Italy as the country with the most top awards.

Funds from the sale of the Marine Corps 230th Anniversary silver dollars benefited the Marine Corps heritage foundation and helped to construct the national museum of the Marine Corps in Quantico, Virginia.

Norman E. Nemeth designed the obverse of the coin. The chosen design copies a photograph by Joe Rosenthal of the United States Marines raising the American flag on Iwo Jima in 1943. In addition to the inscription, "Marines 1775-2005," the obverse contains two mottoes required by law on all United States coins, "In God We Trust," and "Liberty."

The denomination, name of the country and the other third legend required by law to appear on all United States Coins, "E. Pluribus Unum" were inscribed on Charles L. Vickers' reverse design. It features an engraving of an eagle, globe and anchor, the official emblem of the United States Marine Corps.

The commemorative was minted at the Philadelphia Mint in both uncirculated and proof. All 600,000 coins were sold. Because of the high mintage and the care taken to strike these coins at the Mint, they are readily available in high grades of MS69, Proof-69 and better.

MOST HISTORICALLY SIGNIFICANT
Germany, 10 Euro, Silver,
Albert Einstein,
Theory of Relativity

MOST POPULAR
United States, 5 Cents,
Cupronickel, *Bison*

MOST ARTISTIC
Belarus, 20 Rouble, Silver,
Easter Egg

**MOST INNOVATIVE.
BEST
CONTEMPORARY
EVENT**
Australia, 1 Dollar, Silver,
*End of World War II,
Dancing Man*

MOST INSPIRATIONAL
Israel,
2 New Sheqalim, Silver,
*Moses and the 10
Commandments*

BEST GOLD
Germany, 100 Euro, Gold,
World Cup Soccer

BEST SILVER
Austria, 20 Euro, Silver,
S.M.S. Saint George

BEST CROWN
United States, 1 Dollar, Silver,
U.S. Marine Corps

BEST TRADE
United States, 25 Cents, Clad,
Oregon State Quarter

2008

AWARDS

FOR COINS MINTED IN 2006

COIN OF THE YEAR

Canada, 50 Dollar, Palladium, *Ursa Major and Ursa Minor Through the Seasons*

For the first time in the history of the Coin of the Year Award, the winner for coins dated 2006 went to a four-coin set. While this had not been the first time a coin in a set was selected, it is the first time the committee of judges selected a complete set of coins.

The four palladium coins won in the Most Innovative Coin category because of the use of a special laser effect. The judges nominated the four-coin set because the total vision for the coins requires them to be viewed together. The coins illustrate the unique location of Canada's capital where the constellations Ursa Major (big bear) and Ursa Minor (little bear) never disappear from the night sky. They just change locations.

Colin Mayne designed the coins to show the movement of the constellations in the spring, summer, fall and winter. The perspective of the viewer does not change. The landscape on the bottom third of each coin is the same. The four coins viewed together show the complete circle of the constellations in the sky over the course of a single year.

Each coin contains one ounce of palladium. With fewer than 300 specimen coins minted for each of the four coins in this set, it is the rarest and most expensive set of coins to receive the Krause Coin of the Year Award. These coins are seldom, if ever, offered for sale so even when the price of palladium retreats from its current high levels, this set is likely to remain pricy. The set was packaged in a maroon clamshell case lined with flock and protected by a black beauty box.

**MOST HISTORICALLY
SIGNIFICANT**
United States, 1 Dollar, Silver,
*Benjamin Franklin, Elder
Statesman*

**MOST POPULAR,
BEST TRADE**
United States, 25 Cent, Clad,
Nevada State Quarter

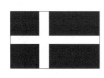

MOST ARTISTIC
Denmark, 10 Kroner, Silver,
*Hans Christian Anderson's
"Snow Queen"*

MOST INNOVATIVE
Canada,
50 Dollar, Palladium,
Ursa Major and Ursa Minor
Through the Seasons

MOST INSPIRATIONAL
Canada,
25 cents, Nickel-Clad,
Pink Ribbon

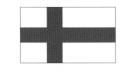

MOST INSPIRATIONAL
Finland, 5 Euro, Gold,
*150th Anniversary
of the Demilitarization
of the Aland Islands*

BEST GOLD
Austria, 100 Euro, Gold,
The Rivergate of Vienna

BEST SILVER
Japan, 1,000 Yen, Silver,
*50th Anniversary
of Japanese Entry into
the United Nations*

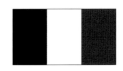

BEST CROWN
France, 1 ½ Euro, Silver,
*Jules Verne's "Five Weeks
in a Balloon"*

BEST
CONTEMPORARY
EVENT
Latvia, 1 Lats, Silver,
Latvian Independence, 1918

PEOPLE'S CHOICE
Hungary, 50 Forint,
Cupronickel,
*50th Anniversary
of the Hungarian
Revolution Against Soviet
Occupation*

2009

---------- **AWARDS** ----------

FOR COINS MINTED IN 2007

COIN OF THE YEAR

Mongolia, 500 Tugrik, Silver, *Wildlife Protection, Gulo Gulo (Wolverine)*

Mongolia won the award for Best Silver Coin with the 500 Tugrik *Wolverine* which was ultimately selected Coin of the Year for coins dated 2007.

The first coin in Mongolia's new Wildlife Series of coins featured an animal on the endangered species list, the wolverine. The National Bank of Mongolia hired CIT to develop, manufacture and sell the coins in the series.

Known for its innovative coin designs, CIT took the challenge to present animals in a new and modern way for the Mongolian series. The wolverine is sculpted to appear as if it is squeezing its way through the rim of a bottle. The rim of the coin is used as a design element to constrain the wolf's face and neck. The high relief enhances the effect.

In order to show the penetrating eyes of the wolf, the artist used crystallized Swarovski inserts that shine light and make the wolf's eyes glisten. The antique finish on the silver deadens the reflectivity of the metal and focuses the viewer's attention on the animal's eyes.

While a mintage of 2,500 is low, the popularity of these coins among collectors has created significant demand. This coin is not likely to be found for less than five times its original issue price. The coins were sold in capsules with an information leaflet. Grading services do not place this coin in a holder due to the crystallized Swarovski insert.

MOST HISTORICALLY SIGNIFICANT
United States, 1 Dollar, Silver, *The Founding of Jamestown in 1607*

MOST POPULAR
United States, 1 Dollar, Copper, Zinc, Manganese, Nickel, *George Washington*

MOST ARTISTIC
Austria, 10 Euro, Silver, *Melk Abbey*

MOST INNOVATIVE
British Virgin Islands,
50 Dollar, Silver, *Centenary of
the First Color Photograph*

MOST INSPIRATIONAL
Belarus, 1,000 Rouble, Silver,
St. Euphrasyne of Polatsk

BEST GOLD
Denmark, 1,000 Kroner,
Gold, Polar Bear

BEST SILVER
Mongolia, 500 Tugrik, Silver,
*Wildlife Protection, Gulo Gulo
(Wolverine)*

BEST CROWN
Belarus, 20 Rouble, Silver,
Pancake Week

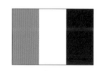

BEST TRADE
Italy, 2 Euro, Bi-Metallic,
Raphael's Dante Alighieri

**BEST
CONTEMPORARY
EVENT**
United States, 1 Dollar, Silver,
*The Desegregation of Little
Rock Central
High School in 1957*

PEOPLE'S CHOICE
Hungary, 5,000 Forint, Silver,
Castle of Gyula

2010

AWARDS

FOR COINS MINTED IN 2008

COIN OF THE YEAR

Latvia, 20 Lati, Gold, *Coins of Latvia*

The nominators at Krause broke with tradition to nominate the Latvia 20 Lati as a candidate for Best Gold Coin. It won the category award and went on to win the Coin of the Year award for coins dated 2008.

Krause judges have generally refused to consider reproductions of unused coin designs from the past. This coin design for a 1922 coin by Teodors Zajkalns was kept at the Latvian National Museum of History as a plaster model. It was never struck. The coin model was finally used in 2008 to celebrate the 15th anniversary of the renewal of the Lats currency following Latvian independence from the Soviet Union.

Zajkalns' obverse portrait of a woman was modeled after an unnamed refugee during World War I. The woman wears a headscarf, signifying motherhood in the Latvian tradition. One of the loose ends of the scarf is tied in a knot because it is said that it helps one remember and that if tied when a star is fallen and a wish is made, the wish will come true.

The narrative from coin's accompanying leaflet explains the symbolism of the reverse as follows:

The feminine principle gives life to an individual and likewise is at the core of the family and state. The feminine principle unites the spiritual with the material; the symbols on the reverse of the coin, bread, apple, vessel with a curdled milk beverage and a jug of milk, also signify fertility and plentitude. A knife, symbolizing masculine action, is placed next to the feminine images.

Only 5,000 of these coins were minted at the Austrian Mint on behalf of the Bank of Latvia. While they are not rare, grades above MS67 are scarce.

**MOST HISTORICALLY
SIGNIFICANT**
Kazakhstan, 100 Tenge,
Silver, *Genghis Khan*

MOST POPULAR
United States,
1 Dollar, Silver,
American Eagle

MOST ARTISTIC
Poland, 200 Zlotych, Gold,
Warsaw Ghetto Uprising

MOST INNOVATIVE
Austria, 25-Euro,
Silver and Niobium,
Fascination Light

MOST INSPIRATIONAL
Canada 2,500 Dollars, Gold,
Towards Confederation

BEST GOLD
Latvia, 20 Lati, Gold,
Coins of Latvia

BEST SILVER
Germany, 10 Euro, Silver,
Fanz Kafka

BEST CROWN
Austria, 10 Euro, Silver,
The Abbey of Klosterneuberg

BEST TRADE
Cyprus, 2 Euro, Bi-Metallic,
Ancient Statue Cross

**BEST
CONTEMPORARY
EVENT**
Israel, 1 New Sheqalim, Silver,
60th Anniversary of Israel

PEOPLE'S CHOICE
Hungary, 5,000 Forint, Silver,
Tokaj Wine Region

AWARDS

FOR COINS MINTED IN 2009

COIN OF THE YEAR

South Africa, 100 Rand, Gold, *White Rhino*

The South Africa 100 Rand *White Rhino* coin won the award for Best Gold Coin and then went on to win the Coin of the Year for coins dated 2009, marking the second time South Africa won the highest honor.

South Africa's gold bullion coin series began its new theme "Safari through South Africa" in 2009 by featuring the white rhinoceros on the "Save the Rhino" project. The white rhino is an endangered species with fewer than 18,000 surviving in the wild. Not more than 100 years earlier fewer than 18 white rhino's remained in existence.

Natanya van Niekerk designed this coin with a strong animal conservation theme. The coin's obverse features a rhino peeking through a silhouette of itself. On the reverse, the animal boldly stomps through its own shadow as if defying extinction. Niekerk blends the country name and denomination into the animal habitat design of fields.

Four denominations with different designs—100 Rand, 50 Rand, 20 Rand and 10 Rand—were issued depicting the white rhino on the obverse and a scene in the life of the rhino on the reverse. They were sold separately, but 400 numbered box sets containing all four denominations were sold along with a silver Rhino figure made exclusively for the box set by Stephen Sutherland.

The coin comes both with and without a privy mark. The coins marked, "EWT" (Endangered Wildlife Trust) are extremely rare with a mintage of only 300. Because of the way they were handled, grades above Proof-63 are rare for coins with the privy mark.

MOST HISTORICALLY SIGNIFICANT
Kazakhstan, 100-Tenge, Silver, *Attila the Hun*

MOST POPULAR
Austria, 10-Euro, Silver, *Basilisk of Vienna*

MOST ARTISTIC
Canada, 300-Dollar, Gold, *Native American Summer Moon Mask*

MOST INNOVATIVE
British Indian Ocean
Territory, 2-Pound,
Silver-Crystal,
Life of the Sea Turtle

MOST INSPIRATIONAL
Poland, 10-Zlotych, Silver,
*World War II Polish
Underground*

BEST GOLD
South Africa, 100-Rand,
Gold, *White Rhino*

BEST SILVER
Canada, 20-Dollar, Silver,
Crystal Snowflake

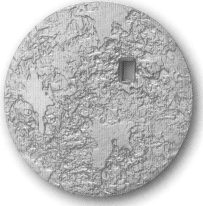

BEST CROWN
Finland, 20-Euro, Silver,
Peace and Security

BEST TRADE
Slovakia, 2-Euro,
Bi-Metallic,
First Year of Euro Issuance

**BEST
CONTEMPORARY
EVENT**
France, 10-Euro, Silver,
Fall of the Berlin Wall

PEOPLE'S CHOICE
Hungary, 5,000-Forint, Silver,
*World Heritage Sites in
Hungary, Budapest*

COIN OF THE YEAR

Israel, 2 New Sheqalim, Silver, Jonah in the Whale

Israel won the Most Artistic Coin Award with its 2 New Sheqalim depicting Jonah in the whale. This striking silver coin went on the win the Coin of the Year for coins dated 2010.

The reverse design by Gideon Keich depicts a whale in relief. Opposite is a proof field. The figure of Jonah with outstretched arms praying for forgiveness is incuse in the belly of the whale from which he rises after three days. Depending on how you view the coin, you can see either a wave engulfing Jonah or a whale with Jonah in its belly. The synergy of the optical illusion suggests a "yin yang" interpretation to the biblical story of Jonah.

Aharon Shevo's obverse design shows the denomination in the center encircled by the bible passage, Jonah 2:1, "Jonah in the belly of the fish," in Hebrew, English and Arabic. At the bottom is a small figure of Jonah in prayer and supplication. The proof 2 New Sheqalim coin bears mintmark, "mem" in Hebrew below the denomination.

Only 2,800 of the 2 New Sheqalim coins were minted, but this coin is available in high grades because of the care taken by the mint in coining and packaging them. The same design appears on a 1 New Sheqel, which is also available in Mint State with the Star of David mintmark. A gold 10 New Sheqalim was also made. These coins were sold as sets in limited quantities.

**MOST HISTORICALLY
SIGNIFICANT**
Canada, 100 Dollars, Gold,
*400th Anniversary of
Hudson Bay*

MOST POPULAR
Austrian Mint,
1.5 Euro, Silver,
Austrian Philharmonic

MOST ARTISTIC
Israel, 2 New Sheqalim, Silver,
Jonah in the Whale

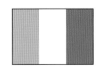

MOST INNOVATIVE
Ivory Coast,
1,500 Francs CFA, Silver,
Mecca Quibla Compass

MOST INSPIRATIONAL
Finland, 20 Euro, Silver,
Children & Creativity

BEST GOLD
United Kingdom,
100 Pounds, Gold,
*Olympic Games
Faster Series Neptune*

BEST SILVER
Austria, 10 Euros, Silver,
Erzberg in Styria

BEST CROWN
Andorra, 5 Diners, Silver,
Brown Bear

BEST TRADE
San Marino, 2 Euros,
Bi-Metallic,
*500th Birth of Sandro
Botticelli*

**BEST
CONTEMPORARY
EVENT**
Germany, 10 Euro, Silver,
German Unification

PEOPLE'S CHOICE
Hungary, 5,000 Forint, *Silver,
Orseg National Park*

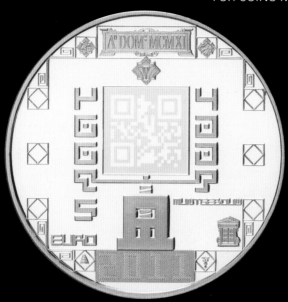

COIN OF THE YEAR

Royal Dutch Mint, 5 Euro, Silver, *100th Anniversary of the Dutch Mint*

Netherlands took the prize for Most Innovative Coin and the prestigious Coin of the Year for coins dated 2011 with its 5 Euro commemorative for the centennial of the Utrecht Mint building. This is the first coin to have a working QR barcode in the design.

Juan Jose Sanches Sastano designed the coin with a two dimensional QR barcode. When a mobile devise equipped with a barcode reader scans the barcode on the coin it takes you to a website with information about the Mint you can read on your device. The bar code sits on top of a screw press, the first mechanical device used to strike coins after they stopped hammering them.

The web page that the QR code used contained a video and a button to a memory coin game. The content of the website can change. For the initial issuance of the coin, proving that the QR code could be used was point enough. The obverse portrait of Queen Beatrix is in the new, modern style with computer modeling and lazar application at the Royal Dutch Mint.

Silver plated copper-nickel coins were sold on cards containing an information booklet about the coin and the mint. Proof coins with a mintage of 12,000 were sold in capsules attached to a blister pack. A 10 Euro gold coin with the same design was also made with a mintage of 3,500 and sold in a wood box. They are not difficult to obtain except in grades over Proof-65.

MOST HISTORICALLY SIGNIFICANT
National Bank of the Kyrgyz Republic, 10 Som, Silver, *The Silk Road*

MOST POPULAR
National Bank of Mongolia, 500 Togrog, Silver, *Ural Owl*

MOST ARTISTIC
Bank of Latvia, 1 Lats, Sliver, *Alexsandrs Caks*

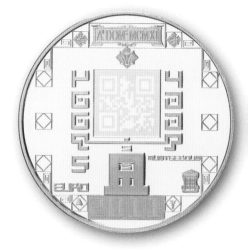

MOST INNOVATIVE
Royal Dutch Mint,
5 Euro, Silver,
*100th Anniversary
of the Dutch Mint
with QR Code*

MOST INSPIRATIONAL
Mint of Poland,
10 Zlotych, Silver,
*100th Anniversary of the
Society for the Protection
of the Blind*

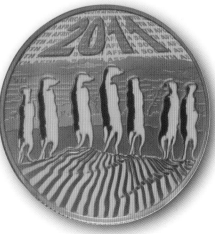

BEST GOLD
South African Mint,
50 Rand, Gold,
*Nature's Families:
The Meerkat*

BEST SILVER
Royal Canadian Mint,
20 Dollars, Silver,
Canoe

BEST CROWN
Monnaie de Paris,
10 Euro, Silver,
From Clovis to the Republic:
Charlemagne

BEST TRADE
National Bank of Lithuania,
1 Litas, Copper-Nickel,
Basketball

**BEST
CONTEMPORARY
EVENT**
Austrian Mint,
25 Euro, Silver & Niobium,
Robotics

2014

AWARDS

FOR COINS MINTED IN 2012

COIN OF THE YEAR

France, 10 Euro, Silver, *Yves Klein*

For the first time in the history of the Krause Coin of the Year Award, top honors went to a coin with coloring. The French 10 Euro coin commemorating Yves Klein won the award for Most Artistic Coin and was selected by the judges as the Coin of the Year for coins dated 2012.

This was the fourth time France won the Coin of the Year Award tying with Italy as the second most honored country. France also won the award for Best Silver Coin for coins dated 2012 with the 10 Euro SS France Ocean Liner, Le France.

Yves Klein (1928-1962) is regarded as one of the most important French artists of the modern era. In 1960 he was among those who founded *Nouveau Realisme*, France's response to the American pop art movement. Klein was also a leader in body art and an early influence in performance art. Klein created a recipe for "International Klein Blue" which became his signature color.

The obverse design shows the bow-tied Klein with his outstretched hand drenched in International Klein Blue. His eyes are penetrating. The color on Klein's hand is an integral part of the coin design. The reverse is a rendition of one of Klein's paintings.

The Paris Mint made this coin in several denominations in both gold and silver. There is a 10-ounce proof silver 100 Euro coin with a mintage of 500; a 5-ounce silver proof 50 Euro coin with a mintage of 500; a 5-ounce gold 500 Euro weighing 5 ounces with a mintage of 99; and a ¼ ounce 50 Euro gold coin with a mintage of 1,000. The 10 Euro silver proof Coin of the Year award winner has a mintage of 30,000 and is not difficult to obtain.

**MOST HISTORICALLY
SIGNIFICANT**
Bank of Greece - Mint,
10 Euro, Silver,
Socrates

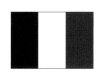

MOST ARTISTIC
Monnaie de Paris,
10 Euro, Silver,
Yves Klein

MOST INNOVATIVE
Royal Canadian Mint, 25
Cents, Nickel-Plated Steel,
*Glow-In-The-Dark
Dinosaur Skeleton*

MOST INSPIRATIONAL
Alderney, 5 Pounds,
Copper-Nickel,
Remembrance Day

BEST GOLD
Istituto Poligrafico e Zecca
dello Stato, 20 Euro, Gold,
Flora in the Arts - Middle Ages

BEST SILVER
Monnaie de Paris,
10 Euro, Silver,
Ocean Liner "Le France"

BEST CROWN
Royal Australian Mint,
5 Dollars, Silver,
Southern Cross in Night Sky

**BEST
CONTEMPORARY
EVENT**
Great Britain,
10 Pounds, Silver,
2012 London Olympic Games

BEST BI-METALLIC
Mint of Finland,
50 Euro, Silver & Gold,
*Helsinki - World Design
Capital*

BEST CIRCULATING
Royal Australian Mint,
1 Dollar, Aluminum-Bronze,
Australian Year of the Farmer

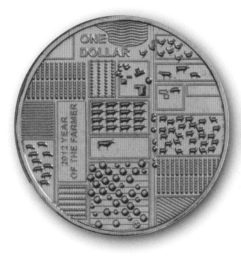

2015

— AWARDS —

FOR COINS MINTED IN 2013

COIN OF THE YEAR

Austrian Mint, 50 Euro, Gold, *Gustav Klimt*

The Austrian Mint won three of the ten categories for coins dated 2013, including the prestigious Coin of the Year for the 50 Euro gold coin, "Klimt & His Women, The Expectation." The spectacular coin celebrating the work of famed artist Gustav Klimt, also won the "Best Gold" category. A 100 Euro gold coin, KM-3225, depicting a Red Deer as part of the Austrian Wildlife series won the "Most Artistic" category. A 25 Euro silver and niobium coin, KM-321, depicting the theme of tunneling won in the "Best Bi-metallic" category.

The 50 Euro gold Klimt, the second in a five coin series celebrating the important artist depicts his painting, "The Expectation" on the reverse.

The reverse, designed by mint engraver Herbert Waehner, depicts a Klimt painting of the face of a young dancer yearning for love. Her hand is held in a pose reminiscent of Egyptian paintings. The letter "L" in the right field is the second letter of Klimt's name which all five gold coins spell when they are assembled.

The obverse design by chief engraver Thomas Pesendorfer, features the "Tree of Life" from the Stoclet dining room in Brussels commissioned to Klimt. His tree bears both flowers and fruit symbolizing man and woman together and on their own. To the right, the image of a falcon interprets the Eye of Horus in the manner of Klimt.

This is the second time Kimpt has been honored as a subject for the Coin of the Year award. In 2003, Austria's 100 Euro depicting Klimt's, "The Kiss," KM-3108, won "Best Gold."

The 50 Euro gold is 22mm, 10 grams gold, struck in proof only with a mintage of 30,000. Grades in Proof 69 should be readily available. Each coin is sold in a box with a numbered certificate. A wood collection case is available for the five coin series.

**MOST HISTORICALLY
SIGNIFICANT**
Royal Dutch Mint
5 Euro, Silver,
1713 Treaty of Utrecht

MOST ARTISTIC
Austrian Mint
100 Euro, Gold,
Austrian Wildlife - Red Deer

MOST INNOVATIVE
Bank of Mongolia
500 Tugrik,
Gold-plated Silver,
Howling Wolf Laser Cutout

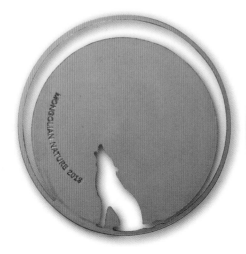 

MOST INSPIRATIONAL
Royal Canadian Mint
3 Dollars, Silver,
*Grandfather and
Grandson Fishing*

BEST GOLD
Austrian Mint
50 Euro, Gold,
Gustav Klimt

BEST SILVER
Bank of Latvia
1 Lats, Silver,
Richard Wagner

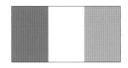

BEST CROWN
Central Bank of Ireland
10 Euro, Silver,
James Joyce

BEST BI-METALLIC
Austrian Mint
25 Euro, Silver & Niobium,
Tunneling

BEST CONTEMPORARY EVENT
National Bank of the Republic of Belarus, 1 Ruble, Copper-Nickel
90th Anniversary of BPS-Sberbank

BEST CIRCULATING
United States Mint
25 Cents, Copper-Nickel
Mount Rushmore National Memorial

Donald Scarinci is the senior partner in one of the largest law firms in New Jersey. He has collected coins since high school and he is considered an international authority in the field of contemporary art medals having assembled one of the largest privately held collections of art medals in the United States.

Scarinci has written and lectured extensively about medallic art and design. He is a Fellow of the American Numismatic Society and serves on the J. Sanford Saltus Award Committee. He also serves on the American Numismatic Association's Numismatic Art Award for Excellence in Medallic Sculpture.

In 2005, Scarinci was appointed by the United States Secretary of the Treasury to serve on the Citizens Coinage Advisory Committee and is now in his third term. He lends his expertise as a nominating judge for the Krause Coin of the Year Award. Most of the photographs in this book are coins from his near complete collection of Coin of the Year award winners in every category.

Index

ALBANIA

KM# 69 10 LEKE (Page 36)
52.50 g., 0.925 Silver 1.5613 oz. ASW **Subject:** 1992 Summer Olympics - Equestrian **Obv:** National arms, value and date below **Rev:** Horse and rider left, relief design

Date	Mintage	VF20	XF40	MS60	MS63	MS65
1991	980	—	—	150	200	240

KM# 62 50 LEKE (Pages 24,26)
168.15 g., 0.925 Silver 5.0007 oz. ASW, 65 mm. **Subject:** 42nd Anniversary - First Railroad **Obv:** Steam locomotive and passenger train emerging from tunnel at left, date at left, denomination below **Rev:** Diesel locomotive and passenger train emerging from tunnel at right, dates below **Note:** Tunnel is a hole in the coin.

Date	Mintage	VF20	XF40	MS60	MS63	MS65
1988	7,500	PF65 275.00				

ALDERNEY

KM# 27 5 POUNDS (Page 79)
28.28 g., Copper-Nickel, 38.6 mm. **Ruler:** Elizabeth II **Subject:** 5th Anniversary Death of Princess Diana **Obv:** Crowned head right **Rev:** Diana accepting flowers from girl **Edge:** Reeded

Date	Mintage	F12	VF20	XF40	MS60	MS63
2002	—	—	—	—	—	13.00

KM# 219 5 POUNDS (Page 122)
28.28 g., Copper-Nickel, 38.61 mm. **Ruler:** Elizabeth II **Subject:** Remembrance Day **Obv:** Head in tiara right **Rev:** Large poppy in color at left, legend at right **Rev. Legend:** THE ELEVENTH HOUR OF THE ELEVENTH DAY OF THE ELEVENTH MONTH

Date	Mintage	F12	VF20	XF40	MS60	MS63
2012	—	—	—	—	—	18.00

KM# 40 50 POUNDS (Page 88)
1000.00 g., 0.925 Silver 29.7394 oz. ASW, 100 mm. **Ruler:** Elizabeth II **Subject:** D-Day **Obv:** Queen's portrait **Rev:** US and British troops wading ashore **Edge:** Reeded

Date	Mintage	F12	VF20	XF40	MS60	MS63
2004	600	PF65 1,200				

ANDORRA

KM# 315 5 DINERS (Page 113)
15.60 g., 0.999 Silver 0.501 oz. ASW, 35 mm. **Rev:** Bear facing

Date	Mintage	VF20	XF40	MS60	MS63	MS65
2010	3,000	PF63 65.00	PF65 75.00			

KM# 151 10 DINERS (Page 62)
31.47 g., 0.925 Silver 0.9359 oz. ASW **Subject:** Europa **Obv:** Crowned arms above "EURO **Rev:** Europa driving quadriga

Date	Mintage	VF20	XF40	MS60	MS63	MS65
1998	25,000	PF65 35.00				

KM# 90 20 DINERS (Page 43)
26.50 g., 0.925 Silver 0.7881 oz. ASW With 1.5 g. 0.917 gold inlay, 0.0442 oz. AGW. **Subject:** ECU Customs Union **Rev:** St. George

Date	Mintage	VF20	XF40	MS60	MS63	MS65
1993 Matte	5,000	—	—	—	95.00	100

AUSTRALIA

KM# 132 25 CENTS (Page 30)
7.78 g., 0.999 Silver 0.2497 oz. ASW **Ruler:** Elizabeth II **Obv:** Crowned head right **Rev:** Wandjina of Aboriginal Mythology **Note:** The center "plug" coin issued with 1 Dollar, KM#131.

Date	Mintage	VF20	XF40	MS60	MS63	MS65
1989	45,000	PF63 25.00				

KM# 99 50 CENTS (Page 27)
15.55 g., Copper-Nickel, 31.65 mm. **Ruler:** Elizabeth II **Subject:** Australian Bicentennial **Obv:** Crowned head right **Rev:** Ship sailing towards gridmarked map of Australia, compass at upper center **Rev. Legend:** AUSTRALIA - 1788-1988 **Shape:** 12-sided

Date	Mintage	VF20	XF40	MS60	MS63	MS65
1988	8,100,000	—	—	12.00	15.00	17.00
1988	106,000	PF63 10.00				

KM# 437 50 CENTS (Page 72)
15.55 g., Copper-Nickel, 31.65 mm. **Subject:** Royal Visit **Obv:** Head with tiara right **Rev:** Australian flag above Canberra Parliament House, British crown at right **Edge:** Plain **Shape:** 12-sided

Date	Mintage	VF20	XF40	MS60	MS63
2000B	5,000	—	—	7.00	9.00

KM# 689 50 CENTS (Page 83)
15.55 g., Copper-Nickel, 31.65 mm. **Ruler:** Elizabeth II **Obv:** Head right **Rev:** Value within circle of volunteer activities **Edge:** Plain **Shape:** 12-sided

Date	Mintage	VF20	XF40	MS60	MS63	MS65
2003B	13,927,000	—	—	3.50	4.50	5.00
2003B	—	PF65 20.00				

KM# 84 DOLLAR (Page 17)
9.00 g., Aluminum-Bronze, 25 mm. **Ruler:** Elizabeth II **Obv:** Crowned head right **Rev:** 5 kangaroos, value **Edge:** Segmented reeding

Date	Mintage	VF20	XF40	MS60	MS63	MS65
1985	91,400,000	—	2.00	4.00	5.00	7.00
1985	75,000	PF65 12.00				

KM# 131 DOLLAR (Page 30)
31.10 g., 0.999 Silver 0.9989 oz. ASW **Ruler:** Elizabeth II **Obv:** Holey dollar with small silhouette of crowned Queen at top dividing legend, value at bottom **Rev:** 2 crocodiles around hole **Shape:** Round with hole in middle **Note:** The "outer ring" coin issued with the center "plug" 25 cents, KM#132.

Date	Mintage	VF20	XF40	MS60	MS63	MS65
1989	45,000	PF65 42.00				

KM# 269 DOLLAR (Page 52)
9.00 g., Aluminum-Bronze, 25 mm. **Ruler:** Elizabeth II **Subject:** A.B. Banjo Paterson - Waltzing Matilda **Obv:** Crowned head right **Rev:** 3/4-length figure of Banjo Paterson on a walkabout with walking stick **Edge:** Segmented reeding **Note:** Mint visitors and at coin shows were allowed to strike a coin for a fee at the following C - Canberra, M - Royal Melbourne Show, S - Sydney Royal Easter Show and B - Brisbane Agricultural Show.

Date	Mintage	VF20	XF40	MS60	MS63	MS65
1995B	74,353	—	—	35.00	45.00	50.00
1995C	156,453	—	—	30.00	38.00	42.00
1995M	74,255	—	—	35.00	45.00	50.00
1995S	82,810	—	—	35.00	45.00	50.00

KM# 590 DOLLAR (Page 76)
31.10 g., 0.999 Silver 0.999 oz. ASW, 40 mm. **Ruler:** Elizabeth II **Obv:** Queen's portrait **Rev:** Aboriginal-kangaroo design with dots **Edge:** Reeded

Date	Mintage	VF20	XF40	MS60	MS63	MS65
2001B Frosted Unc	—	—	—	—	—	35.00
2001B	—	PF65 40.00				

KM# 723a DOLLAR (Page 88)
31.10 g., 0.999 Silver 0.999 oz. ASW partially gilt, 40 mm. **Ruler:** Elizabeth II **Obv:** Head with tiara right, denomination below **Rev:** Kangaroo with semi-circle background **Edge:** Reeded

Date	Mintage	VF20	XF40	MS60	MS63	MS65
2004B Frosted Unc	—	—	—	—	—	65.00

KM# A797 DOLLAR (Page 91)
31.64 g., 0.999 Silver 1.0161 oz. ASW, 40 mm. **Subject:** 60th Anniversary of the End of WWII **Obv:** Bust right **Rev:** Moving image of Dancing Man

Date	Mintage	VF20	XF40	MS60	MS63	MS65
2005	25,000	PF65 85.00				

KM# 1738 DOLLAR (Page 124)
9.00 g., Aluminum-Bronze, 25 mm. **Ruler:** Elizabeth II **Subject:** Year of the Farmer **Obv:** Head with tiara right **Rev:** Stylized farm layout with produce and animals

Date	Mintage	VF20	XF40	MS60	MS63	MS65
2012	—	—	—	5.00	7.00	10.00

KM# 138 5 DOLLARS (Page 35)
31.10 g., 0.999 Silver 0.999 oz. ASW **Ruler:** Elizabeth II **Obv:** Crowned head right, denomination

below **Rev:** Australian Kookaburra sitting on branch facing right, date below **Note:** Special coin fair issues exist.

Date	Mintage	VF20	XF40	MS60	MS63	MS65
1991	300,000	—	—	—	—	37.50
1991	—	PF65 40.00				

KM# 517 5 DOLLARS (Page 71)
Aluminum-Bronze, 38.6 mm. **Ruler:** Elizabeth II **Subject:** Paralympics **Obv:** Crowned head right **Rev:** Wheelchair racer and multicolor logo, small value to right of chair **Edge:** Reeded

Date	Mintage	VF20	XF40	MS60	MS63	MS65
2000	Est. 30000	—	—	—	12.50	15.00

KM# 1853 5 DOLLARS (Page 123)
36.31 g., 0.999 Silver 1.1662 oz. ASW, 38.74 mm. **Ruler:** Elizabeth II **Rev:** Southen Cross in blue sky **Note:** Concave planchet

Date	Mintage	VF20	XF40	MS60	MS63	MS65
2012P	—	PF65 125				

KM# 596 10 DOLLARS (Page 74)
311.04 g., 0.999 Silver 9.990 oz. ASW, 75.5 mm. **Ruler:** Elizabeth II **Subject:** Calendar Evolution **Obv:** Head with tiara right, denomination below **Rev:** Multicolor solar system in center, zodiac symbols in outer circle **Edge:** Segmented reeding **Note:** Illustration reduced.

Date	Mintage	VF20	XF40	MS60	MS63	MS65
ND(2001)	1,802	PF65 375				

KM# 686 10 DOLLARS (Page 82)
311.00 g., 0.999 Silver 9.9889 oz. ASW, 75.5 mm. **Ruler:** Elizabeth II **Obv:** Queen's head right **Rev:** Alphabet evolution design **Edge:** Reeded

Date	Mintage	VF20	XF40	MS60	MS63	MS65
2003P	1,041	PF65 425				

AUSTRIA

KM# 3050 50 SCHILLING (Page 64)
8.15 g., Bi-Metallic Copper-Nickel Clad Nickel center in Aluminum-Bronze ring, 26.5 mm. **Subject:** Austrian Presidency of the European Union **Obv:** Value within circle of provincial arms **Rev:** New Hofburg palace with logo, within circle, date at bottom

Date	Mintage	VF20	XF40	MS60	MS63	MS65
1998	1,200,000	—	—	—	5.00	
1998 Special Unc	100,000	—	—	—	—	5.00

KM# 3057 50 SCHILLING (Page 68)
8.15 g., Bi-Metallic Copper-Nickel Clad Nickel center in Aluminum-Bronze ring, 26.5 mm. **Subject:** Euro Currency **Obv:** Value within circle of provincial arms **Rev:** Euro currency designs within circle, date below

Date	Mintage	VF20	XF40	MS60	MS63	MS65
1999	1,200,000	—	—	—	5.00	—
1999 Special Unc	100,000	—	—	—	—	5.00

KM# 3007 100 SCHILLING (Page 40)
20.00 g., 0.900 Silver 0.5787 oz. ASW, 34 mm. **Obv:** Two half-length figures, 3/4 left, above inscription, value at bottom **Rev:** 3/4 length figure of Karl V in armor, facing 1/4 left, shield above each shoulder **Edge:** Reeded

Date	Mintage	VF20	XF40	MS60	MS63	MS65
1992	75,000	PF65 12.00				

KM# 3046 100 SCHILLING (Page 60)
20.00 g., 0.900 Silver 0.5787 oz. ASW, 34 mm. **Series:** Habsburg Tragedies **Obv:** Standing portrait in uniform of Emperor Maximilian of Mexico **Rev:** Miramar palace and the SMS Nowara

Date	Mintage	VF20	XF40	MS60	MS63	MS65
1997	65,000	PF65 12.00				

KM# 3059 100 SCHILLING (Page 66)
20.00 g., 0.900 Silver 0.5787 oz. ASW, 34 mm. **Series:** Habsburg Tragedies **Obv:** Archduke Franz Ferdinand and Sophie, 3/4 right **Rev:** The Royal couple getting into the car

Date	Mintage	VF20	XF40	MS60	MS63	MS65
1999	50,000	PF65 12.00				

KM# 3068 100 SCHILLING (Page 72)
20.00 g., 0.900 Silver 0.5787 oz. ASW, 34 mm. **Obv:** Celtic salt miner **Rev:** Celtic coin design with mounted warrior **Edge:** Reeded **Mint:** Vienna

Date	Mintage	VF20	XF40	MS60	MS63	MS65
2000	50,000	PF65 12.00				

KM# 3026 200 SCHILLING (Page 51)
33.63 g., 0.925 Silver 1.0001 oz. ASW, 40 mm. **Subject:** Olympic Centennial, 1896-1996 **Obv:** Male and Female figures standing with outstretched arms joined form a circle around Austrian shield, value and date at bottom **Rev:** Ribbon dancer on knees, left, looking up, Olympic logo upper right **Edge Lettering:** CITIUS ALTIUS FORTIUS

Date	Mintage	VF20	XF40	MS60	MS63	MS65
1995	100,000	PF65 22.00				

KM# 2974 500 SCHILLING (Page 16)
24.00 g., 0.925 Silver 0.7137 oz. ASW, 37 mm. **Subject:** 2000th Anniversary - Bregenz **Obv:** Value within circle of shields **Rev:** Two coins on coin, left one with laureate head right, right one with shield of arms, date at bottom **Edge:** Lettered

Date	Mintage	VF20	XF40	MS60	MS63	MS65
1985	341,800	—	—	—	45.00	
1985 Special Unc	46,000	—	—	—	—	45.00
1985	112,200	PF65 45.00				

KM# 2977 500 SCHILLING (Page 19)
24.00 g., 0.925 Silver 0.7137 oz. ASW, 37 mm. **Subject:** 500th Anniversary - First Thaler Coin Struck at Hall Mint **Obv:** Value within circle of shields **Rev:** Crowned figure with scepter, center, small eagle with shield at left, within inner circle, two dates below circle **Edge:** Lettered

Date	Mintage	VF20	XF40	MS60	MS63	MS65
ND-1986	359,800	—	—	—	45.00	
ND-1986 Special Unc	41,200	—	—	—	—	45.00
ND-1986	99,000	PF65 45.00				

KM# 3011 500 SCHILLING (Page 42)
24.00 g., 0.925 Silver 0.7137 oz. ASW, 37 mm. **Obv:** Hallstatt and the Lakes Region, value below **Rev:** Boats on water **Edge:** Lettered

Date	Mintage	VF20	XF40	MS60	MS63	MS65
1993	180,000	—	—	—	45.00	—
1993 Special Unc	31,200	—	—	—	—	45.00
1993	60,000	PF65 45.00				

KM# 3023 500 SCHILLING (Page 51)
13.45 g., Bi-Metallic 0.1542 ASW 5.333 g, .900 Silver center in 0.2572 AGW 8.113g, .986 Gold ring, 30 mm. **Subject:** European Union - Austrian Membership **Obv:** Symbol with Austrian shield at right, value below, within circle **Rev:** Scene of city within circle **Note:** Stars in outer ring are completely punched through.

Date	Mintage	VF20	XF40	MS60	MS63	MS65
1995	50,000	PF65 475				

KM# 3039 500 SCHILLING (Page 56)
24.00 g., 0.925 Silver 0.7137 oz. ASW **Series:** Town Series - Innsbruck Square **Obv:** View of town square, value below, date at bottom **Rev:** Outdoor market scene

Date	Mintage	VF20	XF40	MS60	MS63	MS65
1996	85,000	—	—	—	45.00	—
1996 Special Unc	25,000	—	—	—	—	45.00
1996	50,000	PF65 45.00				

KM# 3049 500 SCHILLING (Pages 61,64)
24.00 g., 0.925 Silver 0.7137 oz. ASW, 37 mm. **Obv:** Interior view of Adimont Abbey Library, value below legend, date at bottom **Edge:** Lettered **Note:** Book printing.

Date	Mintage	VF20	XF40	MS60	MS63	MS65
1998	68,000	—	—	—	45.00	—
1998 Special Unc	17,000	—	—	—	—	45.00
1998	40,000	PF65 45.00				

KM# 3018 1000 SCHILLING (Page 47)
39.80 g., Bi-Metallic 13.18g 0.4178 AGW, .986 Gold center in 26.67g 0.7717 oz. ASW, .900 Silver ring, 40 mm. **Subject:** 800th Anniversary of the Vienna Mint **Obv:** Symbol at center of three circles, two dates above **Rev:** Crowned figure on horseback in center of three circles surrounded by circle of laborers

Date	Mintage	VF20	XF40	MS60	MS63	MS65
ND-1994	50,000	PF65 750				

KM# 2990 2000 SCHILLING (Page 30)
31.10 g., 0.9999 Gold 0.9999 oz. AGW, 37 mm. **Series:** Vienna Philharmonic Orchestra **Obv:** The Golden Hall organ **Rev:** Wind and string instruments **Edge:** Reeded

Date	Mintage	VF20	XF40	MS60	MS63	MS65
1989	351,000	—	—	—	—	BV+4%

KM# 3159 1-1/2 EURO (Page 111)
31.10 g., 0.999 Silver 0.999 oz. ASW, 37 mm. **Obv:** Golden Concert Hall **Rev:** Bouquet of Instruments **Edge:** Plain **Mint:** Vienna

Date	Mintage	VF20	XF40	MS60	MS63	MS65
2008	7,800,000	—	—	—	BV+10%	BV+20%

KM# 3091 5 EURO (Pages 77,78)
10.00 g., 0.800 Silver 0.2572 oz. ASW, 28.5 mm. **Subject:** Schoenbrunn Zoo **Obv:** Denomination within sun design at center, provincial arms surround **Rev:** Building and animals **Edge:** Plain **Shape:** 9-sided **Mint:** Vienna

Date	Mintage	VF20	XF40	MS60	MS63	MS65
ND(2002)	500,000	—	—	—	12.50	—
ND(2002) Special Unc	100,000	—	—	—	—	22.50

KM# 3096 10 EURO (Page 80)
17.30 g., 0.925 Silver 0.5145 oz. ASW, 32 mm. **Subject:** Ambras Palace **Obv:** Palace, denomination below **Rev:** Three strolling musicians **Edge:** Reeded **Mint:** Vienna

Date	Mintage	VF20	XF40	MS60	MS63	MS65
2002	130,000	—	—	—	20.00	—
2002 Special Unc	20,000	—	—	—	—	30.00
2002	50,000	PF65 40.00				

KM# 3146 10 EURO (Page 99)
17.30 g., 0.925 Silver 0.5145 oz. ASW, 32 mm. **Obv:** Melk Abbey view **Rev:** Inner view of the Melk Abbey dome **Mint:** Vienna

Date	Mintage	VF20	XF40	MS60	MS63	MS65
2007	130,000	—	—	—	30.00	—
2007 Special Unc	40,000	—	—	—	—	35.00

Date	Mintage	VF20	XF40	MS60	MS63	MS65
2007	60,000	PF65 40.00				

KM# 3157 10 EURO (Page 105)
17.30 g., 0.925 Silver 0.5145 oz. ASW, 32 mm. **Subject:** Abby of Klosterneuburg **Obv:** Aerial exterior view of church complex **Rev:** Cloister

Date	Mintage	VF20	XF40	MS60	MS63	MS65
2008 Special Unc	40,000	—	—	—	—	35.00
2008	130,000	—	—	—	30.00	—
2008	60,000	PF65 45.00				

KM# 3176 10 EURO (Page 107)
17.30 g., 0.925 Silver 0.5145 oz. ASW, 32 mm. **Series:** Tales and Legends **Subject:** Basilisk of Vienna **Mint:** Vienna

Date	Mintage	VF20	XF40	MS60	MS63	MS65
2009 Special Unc	30,000	—	—	—	—	35.00
2009	130,000	—	—	—	30.00	—
2009	40,000	PF65 45.00				

KM# 3185 10 EURO (Page 113)
17.30 g., 0.925 Silver 0.5145 oz. ASW, 32 mm. **Subject:** Erzberg in Styria **Obv:** Iron Mine **Rev:** Two mermen with cloak **Mint:** Vienna

Date	Mintage	VF20	XF40	MS60	MS63	MS65
2010	130,000	—	—	—	30.00	—
2010	40,000	PF65 45.00				
2010 Special Unc	30,000	—	—	—	—	35.00

KM# 3127 20 EURO (Page 92)
20.00 g., 0.900 Silver 0.5787 oz. ASW, 34 mm. **Obv:** SMS St. George sailing past the Statue of Liberty, denomination below **Rev:** Shipyard at Pola, boat on water **Edge:** Reeded **Mint:** Vienna

Date	Mintage	VF20	XF40	MS60	MS63	MS65
2005	50,000	PF65 50.00				

KM# 3158 25 EURO (Page 104)
16.50 g., Bi-Metallic 6.5g Niobium center in 10g, 0.900 Silver ring, 34 mm. **Subject:** Carl Baron Auer von Welsbach, 150th Anniversary of Birth **Obv:** Lighting gas lamp before Vienna City Wall **Rev:** Head of Welsbach, development of light bulbs

Date	Mintage	VF20	XF40	MS60	MS63	MS65
2008 Special Unc	65,000	—	—	—	—	80.00

KM# 3204 25 EURO (Page 119)
16.50 g., Bi-Metallic 6.5g Niobium center in 10.0g, 0.900 Silver ring, 34 mm. **Subject:** Robotics **Rev:** Mars rover **Mint:** Vienna

Date	Mintage	VF20	XF40	MS60	MS63	MS65
2011 Special Unc.	65,000	—	—	—	—	80.00

KM# 3217 25 EURO (Page 128)
16.50 g., 0.900 Bi-Metallic 0.4774 oz. 6.5g Niobium center in 10.0g 0.900 Silver ring, 34 mm. **Subject:** Tunneling **Obv:** Tunnel boring machine and air vents **Rev:** 19th century tunnel worker and tunnel **Mint:** Vienna

Date	Mintage	VF20	XF40	MS60	MS63	MS65
2013 Special Unc	65,000	—	—	—	—	80.00

KM# 3090 50 EURO (Page 79)
10.14 g., 0.986 Gold 0.3214 oz. AGW, 22 mm. **Subject:** Saints Benedict and Scholastica **Obv:** St. Benedict and his sister St. Scholastica **Rev:** Monk copying a manuscript **Edge:** Reeded **Mint:** Vienna

Date	Mintage	VF20	XF40	MS60	MS63	MS65
2002	50,000	PF65 600				

KM# 3218 50 EURO (Pages 125,127)
10.11 g., 0.986 Gold 0.3205 oz. AGW, 22 mm. **Series:** Klimt and his Women **Subject:** The Expectation **Mint:** Vienna

Date	Mintage	VF20	XF40	MS60	MS63	MS65
2013	30,000	PF65 675				

KM# 3108 100 EURO (Page 83)
16.23 g., 0.986 Gold 0.5144 oz. AGW, 30 mm. **Obv:** Gustav Klimt standing **Rev:** Klimt's painting "The Kiss **Edge:** Reeded **Mint:** Vienna

Date	Mintage	VF20	XF40	MS60	MS63	MS65
2003	30,000	PF65 900				

KM# 3136 100 EURO (Page 96)
16.23 g., 0.986 Gold 0.5144 oz. AGW, 30 mm. **Subject:** Vienna's River Gate Park **Obv:** Bridge over river scene **Rev:** One of two "sculpted ladies" flanking the park entrance **Mint:** Vienna

Date	Mintage	VF20	XF40	MS60	MS63	MS65
2006	30,000	PF65 900				

KM# 3225 100 EURO (Page 126)
16.23 g., 0.986 Gold 0.5144 oz. AGW, 30 mm. **Series:** Austrian Wildlife **Subject:** Red Deer **Mint:** Vienna

Date	Mintage	VF20	XF40	MS60	MS63	MS65
2013	30,000	PF65 900				

BAHAMAS

KM# 155 5 DOLLARS (Page 47)
31.10 g., 0.999 Silver 0.999 oz. ASW **Ruler:** Elizabeth II **Subject:** Golf - Hole in One **Obv:** National arms within 3/4 circle, legend around, date below **Obv. Legend:** COMMONWEALTH OF THE BAHAMAS **Rev:** Golf ball rolling towards cup **Note:** The cup is an actual hole in the coin.

Date	Mintage	F12	VF20	XF40	MS60	MS63
1994	Est. 50000	PF65 65.00				

BARBADOS

KM# 40 10 DOLLARS (Page 14)
28.28 g., 0.925 Silver 0.841 oz. ASW, 42 mm. **Subject:** Dolphins **Obv:** National arms **Rev:** Three dolphins left

Date	Mintage	F12	VF20	XF40	MS60	MS63
1984FM (M)	—	—	—	—	—	—
1984FM (P)	469	PF65 200				

BELARUS

KM# 436 ROUBLE (Page 129)
13.16 g., Copper-Nickel, 32 mm. **Subject:** BPS-Sberbank, 90th Anniversary **Obv:** National arms and geometric pattern **Rev:** Blossomed tree of life

Date	Mintage	F12	VF20	XF40	MS60	MS63	MS65
2013 Prooflike	5,000	—	—	—	—	—	40.00

KM# 53 20 ROUBLES (Page 84)
33.84 g., 0.925 Silver 1.0064 oz. ASW, 38.5 mm. **Obv:** State arms **Rev:** Two Mute swans on water with reflections **Edge:** Reeded

Date	Mintage	F12	VF20	XF40	MS60	MS63
2003	2,000	PF65 250				

KM# 99 20 ROUBLES (Page 90)
31.10 g., 0.925 Silver 0.9249 oz. ASW, 38.6 mm. **Series:** Easter Egg **Obv:** Quilted cross design **Rev:** Decorated Easter egg with inset pink glass crystal

Date	Mintage	F12	VF20	XF40	MS60	MS63
2005 Antique finish	5,000	—	—	—	—	250

KM# 159 20 ROUBLES (Page 101)
33.62 g., 0.925 Silver 0.9998 oz. ASW, 38.61 mm. **Subject:** Festivals and Rites - Maslenica **Rev:** Pancake and syrup

Date	Mintage	F12	VF20	XF40	MS60	MS63
2007 Antique Patina	5,000	—	—	—	—	130

KM# 58 100 ROUBLES (Pages 81,82)
155.50 g., 0.925 Silver 4.6245 oz. ASW, 64 mm. **Obv:** Theater building **Rev:** Two ballet dancers **Edge:** Reeded **Note:** Illustration reduced.

Date	Mintage	F12	VF20	XF40	MS60	MS63
2003	1,000	PF65 750				

KM# 171 1000 ROUBLES (Page 100)
1000.00 g., 0.999 Silver 32.1186 oz. ASW partially gilt, 100 mm. **Subject:** Cross of St. Euphrosyne of Polotsk **Obv:** Church facade **Rev:** Gold-plated pectorial cross **Note:** Illustration reduced.

Date	Mintage	F12	VF20	XF40	MS60	MS63
2007 Proof-like	2,000	PF65 2,000				

BELGIUM

KM# 222 500 FRANCS (500 Frank) (Page 76)
22.85 g., 0.925 Silver 0.6795 oz. ASW, 37 mm. **Ruler:** Albert II **Subject:** Europe: Europa and the Bull **Obv:** Map and denomination **Rev:** Europa sitting on a bull **Edge:** Plain

Date	Mintage	F12	VF20	XF40	MS60	MS63
2001 (qp)	40,000	PF63 45.00	PF65 50.00			

BERMUDA

KM# 93 60 DOLLARS (Pages 53,55)
31.49 g., 0.999 Gold 1.0114 oz. AGW, 35 mm. **Ruler:** Elizabeth II **Subject:** Bermuda Triangle **Obv:** Crowned head right **Rev:** Map, compass and capsizing ship **Shape:** 3-sided

Date	Mintage	F12	VF20	XF40	MS60	MS63
1996	1,500	PF65 1,750				

BOSNIA-HERZEGOVINA

KM# 88 14 EURO (Page 56)
10.00 g., 0.925 Silver 0.2974 oz. ASW **Subject:** Peace **Obv:** National arms above bridge, date below **Rev:** Rose and the word PEACE in many languages, denomination below

Date	Mintage	F12	VF20	XF40	MS60	MS63
1996PM	—	PF65 35.00				

KM# 110 14 EURO (Page 63)
10.00 g., 0.925 Silver 0.2974 oz. ASW **Subject:** Peace II **Obv:** National arms above bridge, date below **Rev:** Dove in flight with PEACE written in many different languages, denomination below

Date	Mintage	F12	VF20	XF40	MS60	MS63
1998PM	Est. 20000	PF65 40.00				

BRAZIL

KM# 652a REAL (Page 80)
7.00 g., Bi-Metallic Stainless Steel center in Bronze Plated Steel ring, 27 mm. **Obv:** Allegorical portrait **Rev:** Denomination on linear design at left, 3/4 globe with sash on right, date below **Edge:** Segmented reeding

Date	Mintage	F12	VF20	XF40	MS60	MS63
2002	54,192,000	—	—	—	3.00	4.00

BRITISH INDIAN OCEAN TERRITORY

KM# 2 2 POUNDS (Page 108)
22.00 g., 0.925 Silver 0.6543 oz. ASW with glass insert, 38.61 mm. **Ruler:** Elizabeth II **Obv:** Small head at top, sea turtle insert **Rev:** Circle of life of the sea turtle

Date	Mintage	F12	VF20	XF40	MS60	MS63
2009PM	Est. 5000	PF63 80.00	PF65 90.00			

BRITISH VIRGIN ISLANDS

KM# 35 5 DOLLARS (Page 10)
Copper-Nickel **Ruler:** Elizabeth II **Obv:** Young bust right **Rev:** Yellow Warblers

Date	Mintage	F12	VF20	XF40	MS60	MS63
1983FM (U)	—	—	—	—	—	50.00

KM# 415 50 DOLLARS (Page 100)
155.52 g., 0.999 Silver 4.9951 oz. ASW, 65 mm. **Subject:** Color photography, 100th Anniversary **Obv:** Bust in tiara right **Rev:** Conjoined portraits right in photo frame

Date	Mintage	VF20	XF40	MS60	MS63
2007PM	—	PF65 275			

CANADA

KM# 635 25 CENTS (Page 95)
4.43 g., Nickel Plated Steel, 23.88 mm. **Ruler:** Elizabeth II **Subject:** Breast Cancer **Rev:** Colorized pink ribbon applique in center.

Date	Mintage	VF20	XF40	MS60	MS63	MS65
2006P	29,798,000	—	—	—	1.50	—

KM# 1252 25 CENTS (Page 121)
12.61 g., Nickel Plated Steel, 35 mm. **Ruler:** Elizabeth II **Subject:** Pachyrhinosaurus Lakusta **Note:** Skelton glows in the dark.

Date	Mintage	VF20	XF40	MS60	MS63	MS65
2012	—	—	—	—	—	100

KM# 149 DOLLAR (Page 20)
23.33 g., 0.500 Silver 0.375 oz. ASW, 36 mm. **Ruler:** Elizabeth II **Subject:** Vancouver **Obv:** Young bust right **Rev:** Train left, dates divided below, denomination above

Date	Mintage	VF20	XF40	MS60	MS63	MS65
1886-1986	125,949	—	—	—	—	10.00
1886-1986	—	PF65 14.00				

KM# 154 DOLLAR (Page 23)
23.33 g., 0.500 Silver 0.375 oz. ASW, 36 mm. **Ruler:** Elizabeth II **Subject:** John Davis **Obv:** Young bust right **Rev:** Ship "John Davis" with masts, rock in background, dates below, denomination at bottom

Date	Mintage	VF20	XF40	MS60	MS63	MS65
1587-1987	118,722	—	—	—	—	10.00
1587-1987	—	PF65 14.00				

KM# 306 DOLLAR (Page 62)
25.18 g., 0.925 Silver 0.7487 oz. ASW, 36 mm. **Ruler:** Elizabeth II **Subject:** 120th Anniversary Royal Canadian Mounted Police **Obv:** Crowned head right **Rev:** Mountie on horseback, dates at left, denomination above **Note:** Individually cased prooflikes, proofs or specimens are from broken-up prooflike or specimen sets.

Date	Mintage	VF20	XF40	MS60	MS63	MS65
1873-1998	79,777	—	—	—	—	18.00
1873-1998	120,172	PF65 29.00				

KM# 270 2 DOLLARS (Page 54)
7.30 g., Bi-Metallic Aluminum-Bronze center in Nickel ring, 28 mm. **Ruler:** Elizabeth II **Obv:** Crowned head right within circle, date below **Rev:** Polar bear right within circle, denomination below **Edge:** Segmented reeding

Date	Mintage	VF20	XF40	MS60	MS63	MS65
1996	375,483,000	—	—	2.50	5.00	45.00

Date	Mintage	VF20	XF40	MS60	MS63	MS65
1996	—	PF65 10.00				

KM# 1485 3 DOLLARS (Page 127)
31.11 g., 0.999 Silver 0.999 oz. ASW, 38 mm. **Ruler:** Elizabeth II **Rev:** Grandfather and grandson fishing from lake dock, dog at their side

Date	Mintage	VF20	XF40	MS60	MS63	MS65
2013	—	PF63 45.00	PF65 50.00			

KM# 145 20 DOLLARS (Page 16)
33.63 g., 0.925 Silver 1.0001 oz. ASW, 40 mm. **Ruler:** Elizabeth II **Subject:** 1988 Calgary Olympics **Obv:** Young bust right, maple leaf below, date at right **Rev:** Downhill skier, denomination below **Edge:** Lettered

Date	Mintage	VF20	XF40	MS60	MS63	MS65
1985	Inc. above	PF60 200				
Note: Plain edge						
1985	—	PF60 35.00				

KM# 945 20 DOLLARS (Page 108)
31.11 g., 0.999 Silver 0.999 oz. ASW, 38 mm. **Ruler:** Elizabeth II **Rev:** Snowflake - light red crystal

Date	Mintage	VF20	XF40	MS60	MS63	MS65
2009	7,004	PF63 95.00	PF65 100			

KM# 1176 20 DOLLARS (Page 118)
7.96 g., 0.9999 Silver 0.2559 oz. ASW, 27 mm. **Ruler:** Elizabeth II **Obv:** Bust right **Rev:** Canoe and reflection **Edge:** Reeded

Date	Mintage	VF20	XF40	MS60	MS63	MS65
2011	200,000	—	—	—	30.00	—

KM# 672 50 DOLLARS (Pages 93,95)
31.16 g., 0.9995 Palladium 1.0013 oz. APW **Ruler:** Elizabeth II **Subject:** Constellation in Spring sky position **Rev:** Large Bear at top

Date	Mintage	VF20	XF40	MS60	MS63	MS65
2006	297	PF65 1,250				

KM# 673 50 DOLLARS (Pages 93,95)
31.16 g., 0.9995 Palladium 1.0013 oz. APW **Ruler:** Elizabeth II **Subject:** Constellation in Summer sky position **Rev:** Large Bear at left

Date	Mintage	VF20	XF40	MS60	MS63	MS65
2006	296	PF65 1,250				

KM# 674 50 DOLLARS (Pages 93,95)
31.16 g., 0.9995 Palladium 1.0013 oz. APW **Ruler:** Elizabeth II **Subject:** Constellation in Autumn sky position **Rev:** Large Bear towards bottom

Date	Mintage	VF20	XF40	MS60	MS63	MS65
2006	296	PF65 1,250				

KM# 675 50 DOLLARS (Pages 93,95)
31.16 g., 0.9995 Palladium 1.0013 oz. APW **Ruler:** Elizabeth II **Subject:** Constellation in Winter sky position **Rev:** Large Bear towards right

Date	Mintage	VF20	XF40	MS60	MS63	MS65
2006	293	PF65 1,250				

KM# 137 100 DOLLARS (Page 7)
16.97 g., 0.917 Gold 0.5002 oz. AGW **Ruler:** Elizabeth II **Subject:** New Constitution **Obv:** Young bust right, denomination at left **Rev:** Open book, maple leaf on right page, date below

Date	Mintage	VF20	XF40	MS60	MS63	MS65
1982	121,708	PF60 950				

KM# 142 100 DOLLARS (Pages 12,13)
16.97 g., 0.917 Gold 0.5002 oz. AGW **Ruler:** Elizabeth II **Subject:** Jacques Cartier **Obv:** Young bust right **Rev:** Cartier head on right facing left, ship on left, date lower right, denomination above

Date	Mintage	VF20	XF40	MS60	MS63	MS65
1534-1984	—	PF60 950				

KM# 287 100 DOLLARS (Page 58)
13.34 g., 0.583 Gold 0.250 oz. AGW **Ruler:** Elizabeth II **Subject:** Alexander Graham Bell **Obv:** Crowned head right, date below **Rev:** A. G. Bell head right, globe and telephone, denomination upper right

Date	Mintage	VF20	XF40	MS60	MS63	MS65
1997	14,775	PF60 475				

KM# 997 100 DOLLARS (Page 111)
12.00 g., 0.583 Gold 0.2249 oz. AGW, 27 mm. **Ruler:** Elizabeth II **Rev:** Henry Hudson, Map of Hudson's Bay

Date	Mintage	VF20	XF40	MS60	MS63	MS65
2010	Est. 5000	PF65 425				

KM# 288 200 DOLLARS (Page 59)
17.14 g., 0.9166 Gold 0.505 oz. AGW, 29 mm. **Ruler:** Elizabeth II **Subject:** Haida mask **Obv:** Crowned head right, date below **Rev:** Haida mask

Date	Mintage	VF20	XF40	MS60	MS63	MS65
1997	11,610	PF60 975				

KM# 403 200 DOLLARS (Page 71)
17.14 g., 0.9166 Gold 0.505 oz. AGW, 29 mm. **Ruler:** Elizabeth II **Subject:** Motherhood **Obv:** Crowned head right, date above, denomination at right **Rev:** Inuit mother with infant **Edge:** Reeded

Date	Mintage	VF20	XF40	MS60	MS63	MS65
2000	—	PF60 975				

KM# 877 300 DOLLARS (Page 107)
60.00 g., 0.583 Gold 1.1246 oz. AGW, 50 mm. **Ruler:** Elizabeth II **Rev:** Summer moon mask, enameled

Date	Mintage	VF20	XF40	MS60	MS63	MS65
2009	—	PF65 2,250				

KM# 1288 2500 DOLLARS (Page 104)
1000.00 g., 0.999 Gold 32.1186 oz. AGW, 101 mm. **Ruler:** Elizabeth II **Subject:** Old town view

Date	Mintage	VF20	XF40	MS60	MS63	MS65
2008	—	PF65 57,000				

CHINA, PEOPLE'S REPUBLIC

KM# 77 5 YUAN (Page 10)
22.22 g., 0.900 Silver 0.643 oz. ASW **Obv:** Building **Rev:** Marco Polo bust, right, facing left, above ships, denomination below, dates at left of bust **Note:** Prev. Y#54.

Date	Mintage	F12	VF20	XF40	MS60	MS63
1983	15,000	PF60 140				

KM# 67 10 YUAN (Page 11)
27.00 g., 0.900 Silver 0.7813 oz. ASW **Obv:** Temple of Heaven, date below **Rev:** Two pandas, denomination below **Note:** Prev. Y#57.

Date	Mintage	F12	VF20	XF40	MS60	MS63
1983	10,000	PF60 550				
1983 Frosted Proof	Inc. above	PF60 570				

KM# 56 20 YUAN (Page 8)
15.00 g., 0.850 Silver 0.4099 oz. ASW **Subject:** Year of the Dog **Obv:** Temple of Heaven, date lower right **Rev:** Dog above denomination **Note:** Prev. Y#38.

Date	Mintage	F12	VF20	XF40	MS60	MS63
1982	8,825	PF60 600				

KM# 1388 20 YUAN (Page 76)
62.21 g., 0.999 Silver 1.998 oz. ASW, 40 mm. **Subject:** Mogao Grottos **Obv:** 8-story building **Rev:** Buddha-like statue **Edge:** Reeded **Note:** Prev. Y#1082.

Date	Mintage	F12	VF20	XF40	MS60	MS63
2001	—	PF65 150				

KM# 72 100 YUAN (Page 11)
31.13 g., 0.999 Gold 0.9999 oz. AGW **Obv:** Temple of Heaven, date below **Rev:** Panda right within circle, date below **Note:** Prev. Y#52.

Date	Mintage	F12	VF20	XF40	MS60	MS63
1983	25,363	—	—	—	—	1,800

KM# 196 100 YUAN (Page 26)
31.13 g., 0.999 Gold 0.9999 oz. AGW **Subject:** Year of the Dragon **Obv:** Temple of Heaven **Rev:** 2 floating dragons **Note:** Prev. Y#175.

Date	Mintage	F12	VF20	XF40	MS60	MS63
1988	10,000	PF60 2,200				

KM# 599 150 YUAN (Page 44)
622.04 g., 0.999 Silver 19.979 oz. ASW **Obv:** Temple of Harmony **Rev:** Two peacocks, denomination below **Note:** Prev. Y#355.

Date	Mintage	F12	VF20	XF40	MS60	MS63
1993	500	PF63 7,500	PF65 9,500			

KM# 1371 500 YUAN (Page 75)
31.10 g., 0.999 Gold 0.999 oz. AGW, 32 mm. **Obv:** Temple of Heaven **Rev:** Panda walking through bamboo **Edge:** Reeded **Note:** Prev. Y#1088.

Date	Mintage	F12	VF20	XF40	MS60	MS63
2001 D	150,000	—	—	—	—	BV+10%
2001	—	—	—	—	—	BV+10%

KM# 1565 2000 YUAN (Page 87)
155.52 g., 0.999 Gold 4.995 oz. AGW, 60 mm. **Subject:** Maijishan Grottos **Obv:** Grotto view **Rev:** Buddha portrait within halo of flying devatas **Edge:** Reeded **Note:** Prev. #Y1206.

Date	Mintage	F12	VF20	XF40	MS60	MS63
2004(y)	288	PF65 14,500				

COOK ISLANDS

KM# 424 DOLLAR (Page 83)
8.50 g., 0.999 Silver 0.273 oz. ASW, 25.1 mm. **Ruler:** Elizabeth II **Subject:** Zodiac Gemstones - Cancer **Obv:** Crowned head above ornamental center **Rev:** Encapsulated emeralds above Crab (Cancer) **Edge:** Reeded

Date	Mintage	F12	VF20	XF40	MS60	MS63
ND(2003)	10,000	PF65 25.00				

KM# 321 2 DOLLARS (Page 63)
42.41 g., 0.925 Silver 1.2614 oz. ASW **Ruler:** Elizabeth II **Obv:** Crowned head right, date below **Rev:** Cook Islands attractions and features, denomination at right **Shape:** 1/3 circular segment

Date	Mintage	F12	VF20	XF40	MS60	MS63
1998	Est. 20000	PF60 50.00				

Note: This coin is part of a tri-national, three coin matching set with Fiji and Samoa

KM# 40 50 DOLLARS (Page 23)
28.28 g., 0.925 Silver 0.841 oz. ASW **Ruler:** Elizabeth II **Subject:** 1988 Olympics **Obv:** Crowned bust right, date below **Rev:** Torch bearer, globe in background

Date	Mintage	F12	VF20	XF40	MS60	MS63
1987PM	20,000	PF60 30.00				

CYPRUS

KM# 75 POUND (Page 88)
28.28 g., Copper-Nickel, 38.6 mm. **Subject:** Cyprus Joins the European Union **Obv:** National arms **Rev:** Map in center with Triton trumpeting through a seashell **Edge:** Plain

Date	Mintage	F12	VF20	XF40	MS60	MS63
2004	3,000	—	—	—	25.00	50.00

KM# 85 2 EURO (Page 105)
8.50 g., Bi-Metallic Nickel-Brass center in Copper-Nickel ring, 25.75 mm. **Obv:** Ancient cross shaped idol discovered in the village of Pomos in the distrct of Paphos. **Rev:** Large value at left, modified outline of Europe at right

Date	Mintage	F12	VF20	XF40	MS60	MS63
2008	25,000,000	—	—	—	5.00	7.00

CZECH REPUBLIC

KM# 1 50 KORUN (Page 44)
9.70 g., Bi-Metallic Brass Plated Steel center in Copper Plated Steel ring, 27.5 mm. **Obv:** Crowned Czech lion left **Rev:** Prague city view **Edge:** Plain

Date	Mintage	F12	VF20	XF40	MS60	MS63
1993(c)	35,001,000	—	—	2.50	7.50	—

KM# 45 10000 KORUN (Page 67)
31.11 g., 0.9999 Gold 1.000 oz. AGW **Subject:** Karl IV **Obv:** Three gothic shields and St. Wenceslas crown **Rev:** Karl IV with 3 coin designs **Edge Lettering:** *CESKA NARODNI BANKA 31.107g*

Date	Mintage	F12	VF20	XF40	MS60	MS63
1999(m)	1,297	PF60 1,800				

DENMARK

KM# 869.1 5 KRONER (Page 33)
9.20 g., Copper-Nickel, 28.5 mm. **Ruler:** Margrethe II **Obv:** 3 crowned MII monograms around center hole, date and initials LG-JP-A below **Rev:** Wave design surrounds center hole, denomination above, hearts flank **Edge:** Reeded **Note:** Large and small date varieties exist.

Date	Mintage	VF20	XF40	MS60	MS63	MS65
1990 LG; JP; A	46,745,000	—	—	—	—	2.50

KM# 951 10 KRONER (Page 94)
31.10 g., 0.999 Silver 0.9989 oz. ASW, 38 mm. **Ruler:** Margrethe II **Series:** Fairy Tales **Subject:** Hans Christian Andersen's Snow Queen **Obv:** Crowned bust right **Obv. Legend:** MARGRETHE II - DANMARKS DRONNING **Rev:** Ice pieces

Date	Mintage	XF40	MS60	MS63	MS65
2006(h)	25,758	—	40.00	—	

KM# 918 1000 KRONER (Page 100)
8.65 g., 0.900 Gold 0.2503 oz. AGW, 22 mm. **Ruler:** Margrethe II **Subject:** International Polar Year 2007-2009 **Obv:** Crowned bust right **Obv. Legend:** MARGRETHE II - DANMARKS DRONNING **Rev:** Polar bear facing, walking on ice flow **Rev. Legend:** POLARÅR 2007-2009 **Note:** Struck from gold from Greenland having a small polar bear to right of denomination.

Date	Mintage	XF40	MS60	MS63	MS65
2007(h)	6,000	PF63 425	PF65 450		

EGYPT

KM# 550 100 POUNDS (Page 11)
17.15 g., 0.900 Gold 0.4962 oz. AGW **Obv:** Denomination, dates and text **Rev:** Bust of Queen Nefertiti right

Date	Mintage	F12	VF20	XF40	MS60	MS63
AH1404-1983	16,000	PF60 900				

KM# 648 100 POUNDS (Page 26)
17.00 g., 0.900 Gold 0.4919 oz. AGW **Obv:** Denomination, dates and text **Rev:** The golden warrior

Date	Mintage	F12	VF20	XF40	MS60	MS63
AH1408-1988	5,500	PF60 850				

FIJI

KM# 78 2 DOLLARS (Page 63)
42.41 g., 0.925 Silver 1.2614 oz. ASW **Ruler:** Elizabeth II **Subject:** Soft Coral Capital of the World **Obv:** Crowned head at left facing right **Rev:** Denomination at right, coral industry scenes **Shape:** 1/3 circle segment

Date	Mintage	F12	VF20	XF40	MS60	MS63
1998	20,000	PF60 50.00				

Note: Part of a tri-nation, three coin matching set with Cook Islands and Samoa

KM# 64 10 DOLLARS (Page 44)
31.10 g., 0.925 Silver 0.925 oz. ASW **Ruler:** Elizabeth II **Subject:** Discovery of Fiji **Obv:** Crowned head right **Rev:** Cameo of William Bligh upper right, long boat with sailors, denomination below

Date	Mintage	F12	VF20	XF40	MS60	MS63
1993	10,000	PF60 35.00				

FINLAND

KM# 62 50 MARKKAA (Pages 15,17)
19.90 g., 0.500 Silver 0.3199 oz. ASW, 35 mm. **Subject:** National Epic - The Kalevala **Obv:** Trees with reflections, denomination at right **Rev:** Stylized waves with figure, dates below

Date	Mintage	F12	VF20	XF40	MS60	MS63
1985 P-N	300,000	—	—	11.00	12.00	13.00

KM# 67 100 MARKKAA (Page 32)
24.00 g., 0.830 Silver 0.6404 oz. ASW **Subject:** 50th Anniversary of Disabled War Veterans Association **Obv:** Home and landscape scene, denomination above **Rev:** Cross superimposed on people, date below

Date	Mintage	F12	VF20	XF40	MS60	MS63
1990 P-M	100,000	—	—	18.00	20.00	22.00

KM# 78 100 MARKKAA (Page 46)
24.00 g., 0.925 Silver 0.7137 oz. ASW **Subject:** Stadium of Friendship **Obv:** Laurel sprig, stylized stadium, denomination above **Rev:** Sprinters, date above

Date	Mintage	F12	VF20	XF40	MS60	MS63
1994 P-M	80,000	—	—	18.00	20.00	22.00

Note: Encapsulated as KM#69 above, but struck to higher proof quality

1994 P-M	15,000	PF60 25.00				

KM# 81 100 MARKKAA (Pages 49,50)
24.00 g., 0.925 Silver 0.7137 oz. ASW **Subject:** 50th Anniversary - United Nations **Obv:** Design, denomination at left, date below **Rev:** Face foreward, dates at right

Date	Mintage	F12	VF20	XF40	MS60	MS63
1995 P-M	40,000	—	—	18.00	20.00	22.00
1995 P-M	3,000	PF60 65.00				

KM# 83 100 MARKKAA (Page 54)
24.00 g., 0.925 Silver 0.7137 oz. ASW **Subject:** Helene Schjerfbeck - Painter - 50th Anniversary of Her Death

Date	Mintage	F12	VF20	XF40	MS60	MS63
1996 T-M	300,000	—	—	—	60.00	75.00
1996 T-M	3,000	PF60 150				

KM# 111 5 EURO (Page 84)
20.10 g., Bi-Metallic Copper-Nickel center in Brass ring, 34.9 mm. **Subject:** Ice Hockey World Championships **Obv:** Summer landscape and denomination **Rev:** Three hockey sticks and a puck **Edge:** Plain

Date	Mintage	F12	VF20	XF40	MS60	MS63
2003M M-M	150,000	—	—	—	25.00	30.00

KM# 123 5 EURO (Page 95)
18.70 g., Brass, 35 mm. **Subject:** 150th Anniversary - Demilitarization of Aland **Obv:** Boat, Dove of Peace on the helm **Rev:** Tree **Edge Lettering:** AHVENANMAAN DEMILITARISOINTI 150 VUOTTA*

Date	Mintage	F12	VF20	XF40	MS60	MS63
2006 M-M	55,000	—	—	—	20.00	25.00

KM# 172 20 EURO (Page 109)
25.50 g., 0.925 Silver 0.7584 oz. ASW, 38.6 mm. **Subject:** Peace and security **Obv:** Two peace doves with a twig

Date	Mintage	F12	VF20	XF40	MS60	MS63
2009K	11,500	PF65 120				
2009K	3,500	—	—	—	32.00	40.00

KM# 153 20 EURO (Page 112)
33.62 g., 0.925 Silver 0.9998 oz. ASW, 38.61 mm. **Subject:** Children's creativity

Date	Mintage	F12	VF20	XF40	MS60	MS63
2010M	10,000	PF65 120				
2010M	3,500	—	—	—	—	100

KM# 180 50 EURO (Page 124)
10.80 g., Bi-Metallic 5.75 g gold center in 5.8 g .925 Silver ring, 27.25 mm. **Subject:** World Design Capital Helsinki 2012 **Obv:** WORLD DESIGN CAPITAL HELSINKI around angular patterns **Rev:** 50 above angular patterns

Date	Mintage	F12	VF20	XF40	MS60	MS63
2012L	5,000	PF65 600				

FRANCE

KM# 1014 FRANC (Page 42)
22.20 g., 0.900 Silver 0.6424 oz. ASW **Obv:** American soldiers storming Omaha Beach **Rev:** Head of Liberty Statue, flags, denomination and date

Date	Mintage	F12	VF20	XF40	MS60	MS63
1993	1,000,000	—	—	—	22.50	27.50
1993	150,000	PF60 35.00				

KM# 1290 FRANC (Pages 73,75)
17.77 g., 0.980 Silver 0.5599 oz. ASW **Subject:** The Last Franc **Obv:** Legend on polished field **Obv. Legend:** UN ULTIME FRANC **Rev:** Number "1" on polished field **Edge Lettering:** REPUBLIQUE FRANCAISE STARCK LIBERTE EGALITE FRATERNITE (2001). **Mint:** Paris **Note:** The coin is intentionally warped and the edge inscription is very faint. Struck at Paris Mint.

Date	Mintage	F12	VF20	XF40	MS60	MS63
2001 Matte	49,838	PF63 150				

KM# 968 5 FRANCS (Pages 28,29)
10.00 g., Nickel, 29 mm. **Subject:** Centennial - Erection of Eiffel Tower **Obv:** Base of tower, denomination above **Rev:** Eiffel Tower, dates at right **Mint:** Paris

Date	Mintage	F12	VF20	XF40	MS60	MS63
1989	9,774,000	—	—	—	6.50	9.00

KM# 1008.1 20 FRANCS (Page 39)
Tri-Metallic Copper-Aluminum-Nickel center, Nickel inner ring, Copper-Aluminum-Nickel outer ring, 27 mm. **Obv:** Mont St. Michel **Rev:** Patterned denomination above date within circle **Edge:** 4 milled bands

Date	Mintage	F12	VF20	XF40	MS60	MS63
1992	Inc. above	—	—	—	15.00	18.00

Note: Open V in outer ring

1992	60,000,000	—	—	—	15.00	18.00

Note: Closed V in outer ring

KM# 1036 20 FRANCS (Page 48)
Tri-Metallic Aluminum-Bronze center, Nickel inner ring, Copper-Aluminum-Nickel outer ring, 26.8 mm. **Subject:** Founder of Modern Day Olympics - Pierre de Coubertin **Obv:** Head left, 'RF' below, torch at right **Rev:** Building at left, denomination and date divided by Olympic logo at right

Date	Mintage	F12	VF20	XF40	MS60	MS63
1994	15,000,000	—	—	—	10.00	12.00

KM# 955b 100 FRANCS (Page 13)
17.00 g., 0.920 Gold 0.5028 oz. AGW **Subject:** 50th Anniversary - Death of Marie Curie **Obv:** Leafy branches divide date and denomination **Rev:** Head right, two dates

Date	Mintage	VF20	XF40	MS60	MS63
1984	5,000	PF65 950			

KM# 982 100 FRANCS (Page 33)
15.01 g., 0.900 Silver 0.4343 oz. ASW **Subject:** Charlemagne **Obv:** Date and denomination divided by monogram, laurel spray below, circle surrounds **Rev:** Stylized head facing

Date	Mintage	F12	VF20	XF40	MS60	MS63
1990	4,950,000	—	—	—	20.00	37.50	42.50

KM# 995 100 FRANCS (Page 36)
22.20 g., 0.900 Silver 0.6424 oz. ASW **Series:** 1992 Olympics **Obv:** Ski jumpers **Rev:** Crossed flame, date and denomination, logo below

Date	Mintage	F12	VF20	XF40	MS60	MS63
1991	90,000	PF60 37.50				

KM# 1048 100 FRANCS (Page 48)
33.63 g., 0.925 Silver 1.0001 oz. ASW **Subject:** 1996 Olympics **Obv:** Head facing, denomination and date below **Rev:** Javelin Thrower **Edge:** CITIUS ALTIUS FORTIUS

Date	Mintage	F12	VF20	XF40	MS60	MS63
1994	250,000	PF60 35.00				

KM# 1025.1 500 FRANCS (Pages 41,43)
31.10 g., 0.999 Gold 0.999 oz. AGW **Series:** Bicentennial of the Louvre **Obv:** Venus de Milo **Mint:** Paris

Date	Mintage	F12	VF20	XF40	MS60	MS63
1993	5,000	PF60 1,850				

KM# 1117 500 FRANCS (Page 51)
17.00 g., 0.920 Gold 0.5028 oz. AGW **Subject:** V.E. Day **Obv:** Victory in Europe date May 8, 1945, denomination **Rev:** Birds in flight above banners, PAX below **Mint:** Paris

Date	Mintage	F12	VF20	XF40	MS60	MS63
1995	5,000	PF60 950				

KM# 1374 1-1/2 EURO (Page 86)
22.20 g., 0.900 Silver 0.6424 oz. ASW, 37 mm. **Obv:** Soccer ball and denomination **Rev:** Rooster and quill **Edge:** Plain **Mint:** Paris

Date	Mintage	F12	VF20	XF40	MS60	MS63
2004	25,000	PF63 55.00	PF65 60.00			

KM# 1450 1-1/2 EURO (Page 96)
22.20 g., 0.900 Silver 0.6424 oz. ASW, 37 mm. **Subject:** Jules Verne **Obv:** Hot air balloon, parrots

at left, native masks at lower left, foliage at right, native huts below, map of Africa in background **Obv. Legend:** CINQ SEMAINES EN BAILON **Rev:** Head of Verne facing 3/4 right at left center, instruments and anchor in curved band **Rev. Legend:** 1828 JULES VERNE 1905 **Mint:** Paris

Date	Mintage	F12	VF20	XF40	MS60	MS63
2006	2,287	PF63 65.00	PF65 75.00			

KM# 1591 10 EURO (Page 109)
27.20 g., 0.900 Silver 0.787 oz. ASW, 37 mm. **Subject:** Europa - Fall of Berlin Wall **Obv:** Brandenburg gate and doves in flight **Rev:** Head facing and flags

Date	Mintage	F12	VF20	XF40	MS60	MS63
2009P	10,000	PF63 37.50	PF65 40.00			

KM# 1802 10 EURO (Page 118)
22.20 g., 0.900 Silver 0.6424 oz. ASW, 37 mm. **Subject:** Charlemagne, 768-814 **Obv:** Cross on orb, right dates at left, value at right **Rev:** Crowned head left **Mint:** Paris

Date	Mintage	F12	VF20	XF40	MS60	MS63
2011	20,000	PF63 50.00	PF65 55.00			

KM# 2079 10 EURO (Page 122)
22.20 g., 0.900 Silver 0.6424 oz. ASW, 37 mm. **Obv:** Trans-atlantic liner France **Rev:** Two winged smoke-stacks, partial porthole **Mint:** Paris

Date	Mintage	F12	VF20	XF40	MS60	MS63
2012	Est. 10000	PF63 45.00	PF65 50.00			

KM# 2087 10 EURO (Pages 120,121)
22.20 g., 0.900 Silver 0.6424 oz. ASW, 37 mm. **Obv:** Yves Klein, blue hand **Rev:** Klein artwork **Mint:** Paris

Date	Mintage	F12	VF20	XF40	MS60	MS63
2012	—	PF63 40.00	PF65 45.00			

GERMANY - DEMOCRATIC REPUBLIC

KM# 139 20 MARK (Page 32)
Copper-Nickel, 33 mm. **Subject:** Opening of Brandenburg Gate **Obv:** State emblem, denomination **Rev:** Brandenburg Gate **Edge Lettering:** 20 Mark (repeated)

Date	Mintage	F12	VF20	XF40	MS60	MS63
1990A	300,000	—	—	7.00	12.00	16.00

GERMANY - FEDERAL REPUBLIC

KM# 187 10 MARK (Page 50)
15.50 g., 0.625 Silver 0.3115 oz. ASW, 32.5 mm. **Subject:** 150th Birth Anniversary - Wilhelm Conrad Röntgen; 100th Anniversary of x-ray **Obv:** Eagle divides date and denomination **Rev:** Hand and X-rayed hand **Edge Lettering:** ERSTER NOBEL PREIS FUER PHYSIK

Date	Mintage	F12	VF20	XF40	MS60	MS63
1995D	6,500,000	—	—		11.50	12.00
1995D	400,000	PF60 15.00				

KM# 201 10 MARK (Page 72)
15.50 g., 0.925 Silver 0.461 oz. ASW, 32.5 mm. **Subject:** 10th Anniversary of Reunification **Obv:** Eagle and denomination **Rev:** Parliament building **Edge Lettering:** WIR SIND DAS VOLK WIR SIND EIN VOLK

Date	Mintage	F12	VF20	XF40	MS60	MS63
2000A	163,000	PF60 20.00				
2000D	3,000,000	—	—	—	15.00	16.00
2000D	163,000	PF60 20.00				
2000F	163,000	PF60 20.00				
2000G	163,000	PF60 20.00				
2000J	163,000	PF60 20.00				

KM# 238 10 EURO (Page 90)
18.00 g., 0.925 Silver 0.5353 oz. ASW, 32.5 mm. **Subject:** Albert Einstein **Obv:** Stylized eagle within circle, denomination below **Rev:** E=mc2 on a sphere resting on a net **Edge Lettering:** NICHT AUFHOREN ZU FRAGEN

Date	Mintage	F12	VF20	XF40	MS60	MS63
2005J	1,800,000	—	—	—	22.00	25.00
2005J	300,000	PF63 28.00	PF65 30.00			

KM# 271 10 EURO (Page 104)
18.00 g., 0.925 Silver 0.5353 oz. ASW, 32.5 mm. **Subject:** Franz Kafka, 125th Anniversary of Birth **Obv:** Eagle **Rev:** Prague Cathedral, writings & portrait **Edge Lettering:** EIN KÄFIG GING EINEN VOGEL SUCHEN

Date	Mintage	F12	VF20	XF40	MS60	MS63
2008G	1,500,000	—	—	—	22.00	25.00
2008G	260,000	PF63 28.00	PF65 30.00			

KM# 290 10 EURO (Page 114)
18.00 g., 0.925 Silver 0.5353 oz. ASW, 32.5 mm. **Subject:** German Unification, 20th Anniversary **Edge Lettering:** EINIGKEIT UND RECHT UND FREIHEIT

Date	Mintage	F12	VF20	XF40	MS60	MS63
2010A	2,100,000	—	—	—	20.00	22.00
2010A	184,200	PF63 23.00	PF65 25.00			

KM# 237 100 EURO (Page 91)
15.55 g., 0.9999 Gold 0.4999 oz. AGW, 28 mm. **Subject:** Soccer - Germany 2006 **Obv:** Round

stylized eagle **Rev:** Aerial view of stadium

Date	Mintage	VF20	XF40	MS60	MS63	MS65
2005A	70,000	PF63 825	PF65 850			
2005D	70,000	PF63 825	PF65 850			
2005F	70,000	PF63 825	PF65 850			
2005G	70,000	PF63 825	PF65 850			
2005J	70,000	PF63 825	PF65 850			

GIBRALTAR

KM# 151 CROWN (Page 42)
Copper-Nickel, 38.8 mm. **Ruler:** Elizabeth II **Series:** Preserve Planet Earth **Obv:** Crowned bust right **Rev:** Stegosaurus

Date	Mintage	F12	VF20	XF40	MS60	MS63
1993	—	—	—	—	10.00	14.00

KM# 963 CROWN (Page 75)
Copper-Nickel, 38.6 mm. **Ruler:** Elizabeth II **Series:** Victorian Age Part II **Obv:** Bust with tiara right **Rev:** Florence Nightingale holding lantern **Edge:** Reeded

Date	Mintage	F12	VF20	XF40	MS60	MS63
2001	—	—	—	—	10.00	12.00

GREAT BRITAIN
(United Kingdom)

KM# 966 50 PENCE (Pages 45,46)
13.50 g., Copper-Nickel, 30 mm. **Ruler:** Elizabeth II **Subject:** 50th Anniversary of Normandy Invasion **Obv:** Crowned head right **Rev:** Boats and planes **Shape:** 7-sided

Date	Mintage	F12	VF20	XF40	MS60	MS63
1994	6,705,520	—	—	—	5.00	6.00
1994	44,649	PF60 7.00				

KM# 981 2 POUNDS (Page 60)
32.54 g., 0.958 Silver 1.0022 oz. ASW **Ruler:** Elizabeth II **Obv:** Crowned head right **Rev:** Britannia in chariot

Date	Mintage	F12	VF20	XF40	MS60	MS63
1997	Est. 35000	PF60 65.00				

KM# 1000 2 POUNDS (Page 68)
32.54 g., 0.958 Silver 1.0022 oz. ASW, 40 mm. **Ruler:** Elizabeth II **Obv:** Head with tiara right **Rev:** Britannia in chariot **Edge:** Reeded **Mint:** British Royal Mint

Date	Mintage	F12	VF20	XF40	MS60	MS63
1999	Est. 100000	PF63 60.00				

KM# 1037 2 POUNDS (Page 84)
12.00 g., Bi-Metallic Copper-Nickel center in Nickel-Brass ring, 28.4 mm. **Ruler:** Elizabeth II **Subject:** 50th Anniversary of the Discovery of DNA **Obv:** Head with tiara right **Rev:** DNA Double Helix **Edge:** Reeded and inscribed **Edge Lettering:** DEOXYRIBONUCLEIC ACID **Mint:** British Royal Mint

Date	Mintage	F12	VF20	XF40	MS60	MS63
ND(2003)	4,299,000	—	—	6.00	12.00	15.00
ND(2003)	43,513	PF63 16.00	PF65 18.00			

KM# 945 5 POUNDS (Page 17)
39.94 g., 0.917 Gold 1.1775 oz. AGW **Ruler:** Elizabeth II **Obv:** Crowned head right **Rev:** St. George slaying the dragon

Date	Mintage	F12	VF20	XF40	MS60	MS63
1985	14,000	—	—	—	—	BV
1985	13,000	PF60 BV				

KM# 997 5 POUNDS (Page 66)
Copper-Nickel, 38.61 mm. **Ruler:** Elizabeth II **Subject:** In Memory of Diana - Princess of Wales **Obv:** Head with tiara right **Rev:** Head right, dates

Date	Mintage	F12	VF20	XF40	MS60	MS63
1999	5,000,000	—	—	—	15.00	18.00
1999	Est. 100000	PF60 20.00				

KM# 1024b 5 POUNDS (Page 80)
39.94 g., 0.9167 Gold 1.1771 oz. AGW, 38.6 mm. **Ruler:** Elizabeth II **Subject:** Queen's Golden Jubilee of Reign **Obv:** Crowned bust in royal garb right **Rev:** Queen on horse left **Edge:** Reeded **Mint:** British Royal Mint

Date	Mintage	F12	VF20	XF40	MS60	MS63
2002	—	PF63 2,100				

KM# 1227 10 POUNDS (Page 123)
155.50 g., 0.999 Silver 4.9944 oz. ASW **Ruler:** Elizabeth II **Obv:** Head with tiara right **Rev:** Pegasus right

Date	Mintage	F12	VF20	XF40	MS60	MS63
2012	—	PF63 225				

KM# 953 100 POUNDS (Pages 21,22)
34.05 g., 0.917 Gold 1.0039 oz. AGW **Ruler:** Elizabeth II **Obv:** Crowned head right **Rev:** Britannia standing **Note:** Copper alloy.

Date	Mintage	F12	VF20	XF40	MS60	MS63
1987	—	—	—	—	BV+12%	—
1987	13,000	PF60 BV+5%				

KM# 1162 100 POUNDS (Page 112)
32.69 g., 0.9167 Gold 0.9635 oz. AGW, 32.7 mm. **Ruler:** Elizabeth II **Subject:** London Olympics, 2012 **Obv:** Head with tiara right **Rev:** Neptune and sailing **Mint:** British Royal Mint

Date	Mintage	F12	VF20	XF40	MS60	MS63
2010	7,500	PF63 1,850				

KM# 956 SOVEREIGN (Page 29)
7.99 g., 0.917 Gold 0.2355 oz. AGW **Ruler:** Elizabeth II **Subject:** 500th Anniversary of the Gold Sovereign **Obv:** Elizabeth II seated on coronation throne **Rev:** Crowned and quartered shield on tudor rose

Date	Mintage	F12	VF20	XF40	MS60	MS63
ND(1989)	Est. 28000	PF60 1,250				

GREECE

KM# 147 50 DRACHMES (Page 20)
9.00 g., Aluminum-Bronze, 27.5 mm. **Subject:** Homer **Obv:** Ancient sailing boat **Rev:** Head left **Edge:** Reeded

Date	Mintage	VF20	XF40	MS60	MS63
1986(an)	12,078,000	—	0.25	0.50	1.00

KM# 209 2 EURO (Page 88)
8.50 g., Bi-Metallic Nickel-Brass center in Copper-Nickel ring., 25.75 mm. **Subject:** 2004 Olympics **Obv:** Discus thrower **Rev:** Denomination and map **Edge:** Reeded with Greek legend and stars

Date	Mintage	F12	VF20	XF40	MS60	MS63
2004	49,500,000	—	—	—	4.00	6.00
2004 Prooflike	500,000	—	—	—		15.00

KM# 248 10 EURO (Page 121)
34.10 g., 0.925 Silver 1.0141 oz. ASW, 40 mm. **Subject:** Greek Culture" - Socrates **Obv:** Socrates (469-399 B.C.) portrait facing left **Rev:** Ancient sayings, national emblem, value and date

Date	Mintage	F12	VF20	XF40	MS60	MS63
2012	5,000	PF63 120				

HUNGARY

KM# 789 50 FORINT (Page 97)
7.70 g., Copper-Nickel, 27.4 mm. **Subject:** 1956 Revolution **Obv:** Holed flag with Parliament building in background **Rev:** Value **Edge:** Plain **Mint:** Budapest

Date	Mintage	F12	VF20	XF40	MS60	MS63
2006BP	2,000,000	—	—	—	3.00	3.50

KM# 661 500 FORINT (Otszaz) (Page 27)
28.00 g., 0.900 Silver 0.8102 oz. ASW **Subject:** World Wildlife Fund **Obv:** Denomination **Rev:** Montagu's Harrier

Date	Mintage	F12	VF20	XF40	MS60	MS63
1988	10,000	—	—	—	30.00	32.00
1988	25,000	PF60 35.00				

KM# 662 500 FORINT (Otszaz) (Page 25)
28.00 g., 0.900 Silver 0.8102 oz. ASW **Subject:** 950th Anniversary - Death of St. Stephan **Obv:** Ancient coin designs above denomination **Rev:** Figure of King Stephen at left and Queen Gisela of Bavaria at right

Date	Mintage	F12	VF20	XF40	MS60	MS63
1988	5,000	—	—	—	38.00	42.00
1988	15,000	PF60 30.00				

KM# 798 5000 FORINT (Page 101)
31.46 g., 0.925 Silver 0.9356 oz. ASW, 38.61 mm. **Series:** Hungarian Castles **Obv:** Walled tower **Obv. Inscription:** MAGYAR / KÖZTÁRSASÁG **Rev:** Gyula castle **Rev. Inscription:** GYULAI / VÁR **Mint:** Budapest

Date	Mintage	F12	VF20	XF40	MS60	MS63
2007BP	4,000	—	—	—	55.00	60.00
2007BP	4,000	PF65 75.00				

KM# 811 5000 FORINT (Page 105)
31.46 g., 0.925 Silver 0.9356 oz. ASW, 38.6 mm. **Subject:** Europa heritage site Tokaj Wine Region **Obv:** Value within grape wreath **Rev:** Tokaj Hill and TV tower **Edge:** Reeded **Mint:** Budapest

Date	Mintage	F12	VF20	XF40	MS60	MS63
2008BP	5,000	—	—	—	—	48.00
2008BP	15,000	PF63 50.00	PF65 55.00			

KM# 815 5000 FORINT (Page 109)
31.46 g., 0.925 Silver 0.9356 oz. ASW, 38.61 mm. **Subject:** Budapest - World Heritage Site **Obv:** Street scene **Rev:** Panoramic view of Danube and Parliament

Date	Mintage	F12	VF20	XF40	MS60	MS63
2009	5,000	—	—	—	—	50.00
2009	5,000	PF65 60.00				

KM# 820 5000 FORINT (Page 114)
31.46 g., 0.925 Silver 0.9356 oz. ASW, 39.6x26.4 mm. **Subject:** Orseg National Park **Obv:**

Butterfly Rev: Traditional rural buildings **Shape:** Rectangle **Mint:** Budapest

Date	Mintage	F12	VF20	XF40	MS60	MS63
2010BP	3,000	—	—	—	40.00	45.00
2010BP	5,000	PF65 55.00				

INDIA-REPUBLIC

KM# 281 100 RUPEES (Page 16)
35.00 g., 0.500 Silver 0.5626 oz. ASW **Subject:** Death of Indira Gandhi - statesperson, 1917-1984 **Obv:** Asoka lion pedestal above denomination **Rev:** Bust right

Date	Mintage	F12	VF20	XF40	MS60	MS63
ND(1985)(B)	—	—	—	160	180	—
ND(1985)B	—	PF60 250				
ND(1985)B Proof, packaged	—	PF60 400				

IRELAND REPUBLIC

KM# 80.2 10 EURO (Page 128)
28.28 g., 0.925 Silver 0.841 oz. ASW, 38.61 mm. **Subject:** James Joyce **Note:** Corrected quote on reverse.

Date	Mintage	F12	VF20	XF40	MS60	MS63
2013	10,000	PF63 65.00	PF65 75.00			

ISLE OF MAN

KM# 1128 60 PENCE (Page 79)
Bi-Metallic Bronze finished base metal with a silver finished rotator on reverse., 38.6 mm. **Ruler:** Elizabeth II **Subject:** Euro Currency Converter **Obv:** Head with tiara right **Rev:** Rotating map with cut out arrow revealing the Euro equivalent of the country's currency to which the arrow is pointed **Edge:** Reeded

Date	Mintage	F12	VF20	XF40	MS60	MS63
2002	15,000	—	—	—	20.00	22.50

KM# 267 CROWN (Pages 31,33)
Copper-Nickel, 38.5 mm. **Ruler:** Elizabeth II **Subject:** 150th Anniversary of "Penny Black" Stamp **Obv:** Crowned bust right **Rev:** Crowned head left within stamp **Note:** Struck in "pearl black" Copper-Nickel.

Date	Mintage	F12	VF20	XF40	MS60	MS63
1990	—	—	—	—	12.50	13.50
1990	50,000	PF60 16.50				

KM# 275 CROWN (Page 32)
Copper-Nickel, 38.5 mm. **Ruler:** Elizabeth II **Obv:** Crowned bust right **Rev:** Alley cat

Date	Mintage	F12	VF20	XF40	MS60	MS63
1990	—	—	—	—	12.00	16.00
1990	250	PF60 35.00				

KM# 139 ANGEL (Page 14)
33.93 g., 0.917 Gold 1.0003 oz. AGW **Ruler:** Elizabeth II **Obv:** Young bust right **Rev:** Archangel Michael slaying dragon left

Date	Mintage	F12	VF20	XF40	MS60	MS63
1984	—	—	—	—		1,725
1984	3,000	PF60 1,750				

ISRAEL

KM# 441 NEW SHEQEL (Page 105)
14.40 g., 0.925 Silver 0.4282 oz. ASW, 30 mm. **Series:** Independence Day **Subject:** Israel's Sixtieth Anniversary **Obv:** Value, state emblem and inscriptions including "Independence Day **Rev:** 60" the zero is shaped like a pomegranite and a dove

Date	Mintage	F12	VF20	XF40	MS60	MS63
JE5768-2008(v) Prooflike	1,800	—	—	—	—	60.00

KM# 200 2 NEW SHEQALIM (Page 29)
28.80 g., 0.850 Silver 0.787 oz. ASW, 37 mm. **Subject:** 41st Anniversary of Independence **Obv:** Value to left within horizontal lines **Rev:** Roe deer facing right among trees

Date	Mintage	F12	VF20	XF40	MS60	MS63
JE5749-1989(f)	7,062	PF60 40.00				

KM# 311 2 NEW SHEQALIM (Page 64)
28.80 g., 0.925 Silver 0.8565 oz. ASW, 38.7 mm. **Series:** Independence Day **Subject:** 50th Anniversary of Independence **Obv:** Value to right of menorah flanked by sprigs above text **Rev:** Flag within stars

Date	Mintage	F12	VF20	XF40	MS60	MS63
JE5758-1998(u)	8,279	PF60 50.00				

KM# 400 2 NEW SHEQALIM (Page 91)
28.80 g., 0.925 Silver 0.8565 oz. ASW, 38.7 mm. **Series:** Biblical Art **Subject:** Moses and the Ten Commandments **Obv:** Ten Commandments and value **Rev:** Moses and Ten Commandments

Date	Mintage	F12	VF20	XF40	MS60	MS63
JE5765-2005(u)	1,400	PF65 100				

KM# 476 2 NEW SHEQALIM (Pages 110,111)
28.80 g., 0.925 Silver 0.8565 oz. ASW, 38.7 mm. **Series:** Biblical Art **Subject:** Jonah in the Whale **Obv:** Small image of Jonah, value, state emblem **Rev:** Stylized Jonah in belly of whale **Edge:** Reeded

Date	Mintage	F12	VF20	XF40	MS60	MS63
JE5770-2010(v)	Est. 2800	PF65 120				

KM# 286 30 NEW SHEQALIM (Page 54)
155.52 g., 0.999 Silver 4.995 oz. ASW, 65 mm. **Series:** Independence Day **Subject:** Jerusalem's Third Millennium **Obv:** State arms left of value **Rev:** Inscription at center **Edge:** Reeded **Note:** Illustration reduced.

Date	Mintage	F12	VF20	XF40	MS60	MS63
JE5756-1996(f)	2,929	PF60 275				

ITALY

KM# 147 500 LIRE (Pages 34,35)
15.00 g., 0.835 Silver 0.4027 oz. ASW **Subject:** 2100th Anniversary of Ponte Milvio **Obv:** Head right with bridge and shield within hair **Rev:** Stone arch bridge

Date	Mintage	F12	VF20	XF40	MS60	MS63
1991R	59,000	—	—	—	30.00	—
1991R	14,000	PF60 40.00				

KM# 154 500 LIRE (Pages 37,38)
15.00 g., 0.835 Silver 0.4027 oz. ASW **Subject:** Flora and Fauna **Obv:** Head left with bird and flora within hair **Rev:** Square enclosing dolphin, flamingo and other animals

Date	Mintage	F12	VF20	XF40	MS60	MS63
1992R	43,000	—	—	—	30.00	—
1992R	8,500	PF60 60.00				

KM# 169 1000 LIRE (Page 48)
14.60 g., 0.835 Silver 0.3919 oz. ASW **Obv:** Tintoretto in oval **Rev:** Collage of his paintings

Date	Mintage	F12	VF20	XF40	MS60	MS63
1994R	45,000	—	—	—	130	—
1994R	8,500	PF60 170				

KM# 198 5000 LIRE (Pages 65,66)
18.00 g., 0.835 Silver 0.4832 oz. ASW **Subject:** 1999 **Obv:** Three birds and nine stars encircle world **Rev:** Satellite dish and wheels

Date	Mintage	F12	VF20	XF40	MS60	MS63
1999R	—	PF60 60.00				
1999R	37,600	—	—	—	45.00	—

KM# 217 2 EURO (Page 101)
8.50 g., Bi-Metallic Nickel-Brass center in Copper-Nickel ring, 25.75 mm. **Obv:** Bust of Dante Aligheri left **Rev:** Value and map within circle **Edge:** Reeded **Edge Lettering:** 2's and stars

Date	Mintage	F12	VF20	XF40	MS60	MS63
2007R	5,000,000	—	—	—	3.00	—
2007R	12,000	PF63 20.00				

KM# 239 5 EURO (Pages 85,86)
18.00 g., 0.925 Silver 0.5353 oz. ASW, 32 mm. **Subject:** Madam Butterfly **Obv:** La Scala Opera House, where Madam Butterfly was first performed there in 1904 **Rev:** Geisha

Date	Mintage	F12	VF20	XF40	MS60	MS63
2004R	30,000	—	—	—	35.00	—
2004R	12,000	PF63 40.00				

KM# 352 20 EURO (Page 122)
6.45 g., 0.900 Gold 0.1867 oz. AGW, 21 mm. **Subject:** Flora in Art - Middle ages **Obv:** Face at center of triskles **Rev:** Two peacocks face-to-face

Date	Mintage	F12	VF20	XF40	MS60	MS63
2012R	1,500	PF63 650				

IVORY COAST

KM# 7 1500 FRANCS (Page 112)
273.00 g., 0.925 Silver 8.1189 oz. ASW, 50 mm. **Subject:** Qibia Compass **Obv:** National arms **Rev:** Legend and design around center disc for compass spoon

Date	Mintage	F12	VF20	XF40	MS60	MS63
2010 Antique patina	—	—	—	—	500	—

JAPAN

Y# 90 500 YEN (Page 20)
13.00 g., Copper-Nickel, 30 mm. **Ruler:** Hirohito **Subject:** 60 Years of Reign of Hirohito **Obv:** Large chrysanthemum with legends around border **Rev:** Shishinden Palace

Date	Mintage	VG8	F12	VF20	XF40	MS63
Yr.61(1986)	50,000,000	—	—	—	8.00	12.00

Y# 125 500 YEN (Page 71)
7.00 g., Nickel-Brass, 26.5 mm. **Ruler:** Akihito **Obv:** Pawlownia flower and highlighted legends **Rev:** Value with latent zeros **Edge:** Slanted reeding

Date	Mintage	F12	VF20	XF40	MS60	MS63
Yr.12(2000)	595,743,000	—	—	—	7.00	9.00
Yr.12(2000)	226,000	PF60 22.00				

Y# 138 1000 YEN (Page 96)
31.10 g., 1.000 Silver 0.9999 oz. ASW, 40 mm. **Ruler:** Akihito **Subject:** 50th Anniversary of Japan's Entry into the United Nations **Obv:** Globe and plum blossom wreath (enameled blue, pink and green) **Rev:** UN emblem

Date	Mintage	F12	VF20	XF40	MS60	MS63
Yr.18(2006)	70,000	PF65 165				

Y# 92 100000 YEN (Page 20)
20.00 g., 1.000 Gold 0.643 oz. AGW, 30 mm. **Ruler:** Hirohito **Subject:** 60 Years - Reign of Hirohito **Obv:** Large chrysanthemum with legends around border **Rev:** Pair of birds within artistic design

Date	Mintage	VG8	F12	VF20	XF40	MS63
Yr.61(1986)	10,000,000	—	—	BV	950	1,200

Y# 105 100000 YEN (Page 36)
30.00 g., 1.000 Gold 0.9645 oz. AGW, 33 mm. **Ruler:** Akihito **Subject:** Enthronement of Emperor Akihito **Obv:** Chrysanthemum within wreath **Rev:** Stylized Green Phoenix

Date	Mintage	VG8	F12	VF20	XF40	MS63
Yr.3(1990)	1,900,000	—	—	BV	1,500	1,800
Yr.3(1990) (1991)	100,000	PF60 1,900				

KAZAKHSTAN

KM# 110 100 TENGE (Page 103)
31.11 g., 0.925 Silver 0.925 oz. ASW, 38.61 mm. **Subject:** Chingis Khan **Rev:** Khan on horseback facing

Date	Mintage	F12	VF20	XF40	MS60	MS63
2008	13,000	PF63 55.00	PF65 65.00			

KM# 125 100 TENGE (Page 107)
31.11 g., 0.925 Silver 0.925 oz. ASW, 38.61 mm. **Subject:** Attila the Hun **Rev:** Medallic Profile right

Date	Mintage	F12	VF20	XF40	MS60	MS63
2009	13,000	PF63 65.00	PF65 75.00			

KIRIBATI

KM# 22 5 DOLLARS (Page 59)
15.55 g., 0.925 Silver 0.4625 oz. ASW **Subject:** Guerra & Paz **Obv:** National arms within wave-like designs **Rev:** Dove within wave-like designs **Shape:** Jagged half of coin **Note:** Half of two-part coin, combined with Samoa KM#115, issued in sets only. Value is determined by combining the two parts.

Date	Mintage	F12	VF20	XF40	MS60	MS63
ND(1997)	Est. 10000	PF65 35.00				

KYRGYZSTAN

KM# 48 10 SOM (Page 116)
31.10 g., 0.925 Silver 0.9249 oz. ASW partially gilt, 38.6 mm. **Subject:** Great Silk Road **Obv:** National arms above caravan riding right **Rev:** Skyline views and Silk Road map of Eurasia, color logo at top **Edge:** Reeded

Date	Mintage	F12	VF20	XF40	MS60	MS63
2011	Est. 2000	PF65 75.00				

LATVIA

KM# 39 LATS (Page 67)
15.20 g., 0.925 Silver 0.452 oz. ASW **Subject:** Millennium **Obv:** Date divides holes within circle **Rev:** Vertical holes within circle, date on bottom **Note:** Button design.

Date	Mintage	F12	VF20	XF40	MS60	MS63
1999-2000 (1999)	—	PF60 55.00				

KM# 52 LATS (Page 78)
31.47 g., 0.925 Silver 0.9359 oz. ASW, 38.6 mm. **Subject:** Destiny **Obv:** Stylized design **Rev:** Apple tree and landscape **Edge:** Plain

Date	Mintage	F12	VF20	XF40	MS60	MS63
2002	Est. 5000	PF65 150				

KM# 82 LATS (Page 97)
31.47 g., 0.925 Silver 0.9359 oz. ASW, 38.61 mm. **Subject:** Fight for Freedom **Obv:** Outline of Latvia with three stars above **Obv. Inscription:** LATVIJAS REPUBLIKA **Rev:** Two crossed swords outlined against the sun **Rev. Inscription:** NO ZOBENA SAULE LECA **Edge:** Plain

Date	Mintage	F12	VF20	XF40	MS60	MS63
2006	Est. 5000	PF65 65.00				

KM# 126 LATS (Page 116)
Bi-Metallic Granite center in .925 Silver ring, 35 mm. **Subject:** Granite Stone **Obv:** Country name at top, denomination at bottom **Rev:** National folk ornamentation

Date	Mintage	F12	VF20	XF40	MS60	MS63
2011	7,000	PF65 75.00				

KM# 140 LATS (Page 127)
22.00 g., 0.925 Silver 0.6543 oz. ASW, 35 mm. **Subject:** Richard Wagner, 200th Anniversary of Birth **Obv:** Profile left, horn flowing into flower **Rev:** Ship in stormy seas **Edge:** Lettered

Date	Mintage	F12	VF20	XF40	MS60	MS63
2013	—	PF65 25.00				

KM# 96 20 LATI (Pages 102,104)
10.00 g., 0.999 Gold 0.3212 oz. AGW, 22 mm. **Obv:** Woman's head covered with scarf **Rev:** Vessel with a milk bottle, apple, jug of milk, bread & knife on table

Date	Mintage	F12	VF20	XF40	MS60	MS63	MS65
2008	5,000					750	850

LIBERIA

KM# 611 10 DOLLARS (Page 87)
62.21 g., 0.999 Silver 1.998 oz. ASW, 50 mm. **Obv:** National arms left of window design with Tiffany Glass inlay **Rev:** Window design with Tiffany Glass inlay **Edge:** Plain

Date	Mintage	F12	VF20	XF40	MS60	MS63	MS65
2004	999	—	—	—	—	200	—

LITHUANIA

KM# 177 LITAS (Page 119)
6.25 g., Copper-Nickel, 22.3 mm. **Subject:** European Basketball Championship **Obv:** National arms **Rev:** Basketball **Rev. Legend:** EUROPOS KREPSINIO CEMPIONATAS **Edge:** Reeded

Date	Mintage	F12	VF20	XF40	MS60	MS63	MS65
2011	1,000,000	—	—	—	3.00	6.00	9.00

KM# 124 50 LITЦ (Page 70)
28.28 g., 0.925 Silver 0.841 oz. ASW, 38.61 mm. **Series:** XXVII Summer Olympic Games **Obv:** National arms within lined diagonal design **Rev:** Man throwing discus, Olympic emblem and date **Edge Lettering:** NUGALI STIPRUS DVASIA IR KUNU

Date	Mintage	F12	VF20	XF40	MS60	MS63
2000	—	PF60 45.00				

MEXICO

KM# 639 ONZA (Troy Ounce of Silver) (Page 72)
31.10 g., 0.999 Silver 0.9989 oz. ASW, 40 mm. **Subject:** Libertad **Obv:** National arms, eagle left within center of past and present arms **Rev:** Winged Victory **Edge:** Reeded

Date	Mintage	F12	VF20	XF40	MS60	MS63
2000Mo	340,000	—	—	—	—	55.00
2000Mo	1,600	PF63 140				

MONGOLIA

KM# 212 500 TUGRIK (Pags 98,100)
31.11 g., 0.999 Silver 0.999 oz. ASW, 38 mm. **Obv:** Arms and value **Rev:** Wolverine head facing with diamonds in eyes **Rev. Inscription:** WILDLIFE PROTECTION GULO GULO

Date	Mintage	F12	VF20	XF40	MS60	MS63
2007	—	—	—	—	—	1,350

KM# 309 500 TUGRIK (Page 116)
31.10 g., 0.925 Silver 0.9249 oz. ASW, 38.6 mm. **Subject:** Endangered Wildlife **Obv:** National Emblem **Rev:** Owl's head facing (Strix Uralensis) crystal insert eyes

Date	Mintage	F12	VF20	XF40	MS60	MS63
2011 Antique finish	2,500	—	—	—	—	650

KM# 327 500 TUGRIK (Page 126)
16.81 g., 0.925 Silver 0.4999 oz. ASW Gilt, 38.61 mm. **Obv:** Howling wolf seated right, crescent above, State emblem at left **Note:** Laser cut-out

CM Date	Host Date	F12	VF20	XF40	MS60	MS63
2013 Matte proof	2,500	PF65 200				

NETHERLANDS

KM# 308 5 EURO (Pages 115,117)
15.50 g., 0.925 Silver 0.461 oz. ASW, 33 mm. **Ruler:** Beatrix **Subject:** Mint building, 100th Anniversary **Obv:** Bust facing **Rev:** Screw press and a QR-code which is able to be scanned with a mobile telephone **Edge Lettering:** GOD * ZIJ * MET * ONS *

Date	Mintage	F12	VF20	XF40	MS60	MS63
2011	17,500	PF63 40.00				

KM# 326 5 EURO (Page 126)
15.50 g., 0.925 Silver 0.461 oz. ASW, 33 mm. **Ruler:** Beatrix **Subject:** 1713 Peace Treaty of Utrecht

Date	Mintage	F12	VF20	XF40	MS60	MS63
2013	6,500	PF63 60.00				

NEW ZEALAND

KM# 141 DOLLAR (Page 82)
28.28 g., Aluminum-Bronze, 38.61 mm. **Ruler:** Elizabeth II **Subject:** Lord of the Rings **Obv:** Head with tiara right **Rev:** Inscribed ring around value **Edge:** Reeded

Date	Mintage	F12	VF20	XF40	MS60	MS63	MS65
2003(I)	30,081	—	—	—	—	15.00	18.00

Note: Mintage includes 10,454 in sets.

PANAMA

KM# 80 20 BALBOAS (Page 8)
119.88 g., 0.500 Silver 1.9271 oz. ASW, 61 mm. **Subject:** Balboa - Discoverer of the Pacific **Obv:** National coat of arms **Rev:** Standing armored figures **Note:** Illustration reduced.

Date	Mintage	F12	VF20	XF40	MS60	MS63
1982 (P)	2,352	PF60 275				

KM# 98 20 BALBOAS (Page 14)
119.88 g., 0.500 Silver 1.9271 oz. ASW, 61 mm. **Obv:** National coat of arms **Rev:** Balboa and Indian guide **Note:** Illustration reduced.

Date	Mintage	F12	VF20	XF40	MS60	MS63
1984 (P)	1,760	PF60 230	PF63 250			

POLAND

Y# 331 2 ZŁOTE (Page 60)
8.15 g., Brass, 27 mm. **Obv:** Crowned eagle with wings open **Rev:** Zamek W Pieskowej Skale

Date	Mintage	F12	VF20	XF40	MS60	MS63
1997	315,000			9.00	15.00	25.00

Y# 708 10 ZŁOTYCH (Page 108)
14.14 g., 0.925 Silver 0.4205 oz. ASW, 32 mm. **Subject:** Polish Underground State **Obv:** National arms and monogram and cloth flag **Rev:** Figure and cloth flag

Date	Mintage	F12	VF20	XF40	MS60	MS63
2009MW	50,000	PF63 25.00	PF65 35.00			

Y# 796 10 ZŁOTYCH (Page 117)
14.14 g., 0.925 Silver 0.4205 oz. ASW, 32 mm. **Subject:** Society for the Protection of the Blind, 100th Anniversary

Date	Mintage	F12	VF20	XF40	MS60	MS63
2011MW	50,000	PF63 35.00	PF65 45.00			

Y# 498 20 ZŁOTYCH (Page 87)
28.28 g., 0.925 Silver 0.841 oz. ASW, 38.6 mm. **Subject:** Lodz Ghetto (1940-1944) **Obv:** Silhouette on wall **Rev:** Child with a pot **Edge:** Plain

Date	Mintage	F12	VF20	XF40	MS60	MS63	MS65
2004MW Matte	64,000	—	—	—	—	40.00	45.00

Y# 664 200 ZŁOTYCH (Page 103)
15.50 g., 0.900 Gold 0.4485 oz. AGW, 27 mm. **Subject:** Warsaw Ghetto **Obv:** Building on fire, Naitonal arms **Rev:** Face looking out from broken brick wall

Date	Mintage	F12	VF20	XF40	MS60	MS63
2008MW	12,000	PF65 850				

Y# 245 300000 ZŁOTYCH (Page 43)
31.16 g., 0.925 Silver 0.9267 oz. ASW, 40 mm. **Subject:** 50th Anniversary of Warsaw Ghetto Uprising **Obv:** Imperial eagle above value **Rev:** Outreached arms above bricks

Date	Mintage	F12	VF20	XF40	MS60	MS63
1993	30,000	PF60 50.00	PF63 55.00	PF65 65.00		

Y# 269 300000 ZŁOTYCH (Page 47)
31.10 g., 0.999 Silver 0.999 oz. ASW, 40 mm. **Subject:** Warsaw Uprising **Obv:** Imperial eagle above value **Rev:** Fighting soldiers, dates, designs and cross

Date	Mintage	F12	VF20	XF40	MS60	MS63
1994	30,000	PF60 50.00	PF63 60.00	PF65 75.00		

PORTUGAL

KM# 655 200 ESCUDOS (Page 36)
9.80 g., Bi-Metallic Copper-Nickel center in Aluminum-Bronze ring, 28 mm. **Obv:** Shield within globe above value **Obv. Legend:** REPUBLICA PORTUGUESA **Rev:** Armored 1/2 length bust right holding flower within circle **Rev. Legend:** GARCIA DE ORTA **Edge:** Segmented reeding

Date	Mintage	F12	VF20	XF40	MS60	MS63
1991	33,000,000			1.25	3.00	4.00
1991	—	PF60 110				

KM# 712 200 ESCUDOS (Page 62)
Copper-Nickel, 36 mm. **Subject:** India 1498 **Obv:** Shield and sailing ship **Rev:** Ship and coastal map of India

Date	Mintage	F12	VF20	XF40	MS60	MS63	MS65
1998	—				5.00	6.00	7.00

KM# 707 1000 ESCUDOS (Page 64)
27.00 g., 0.500 Silver 0.434 oz. ASW, 40 mm. **Subject:** International Year of the Oceans Expo 98 **Obv:** Shield and logo **Rev:** Stylized expo designs

Date	Mintage	F12	VF20	XF40	MS60	MS63	MS65
1998	1,000,000	—	—	—	20.00	22.50	25.00

RUSSIA

Y# 303 ROUBLE (Page 38)
Copper-Nickel, 31 mm. **Subject:** Rebirth of Russian Sovereignty and Democracy **Obv:** Tower and steeples, value below **Rev:** Winged Victory and small building with flag on top

Date	Mintage	F12	VF20	XF40	MS60	MS63	MS65
1992(l)	700,000				2.50	3.50	5.00
1992(l)	—	PF63 6.00		PF65 8.00			

Y# 262 3 ROUBLES (Page 35)
34.56 g., 0.900 Silver 1.000 oz. ASW **Obv:** National arms with CCCP and value below **Rev:** Yuri Gagarin Monument

Date	Mintage	F12	VF20	XF40	MS60	MS63
1991 (l)	35,000	PF60 45.00				

Y# 250 25 ROUBLES (Page 33)
31.10 g., 0.999 Palladium 0.9989 oz. APW **Subject:** 500th Anniversary of Russian State **Obv:** National arms with CCCP and value below **Rev:** Peter the Great

Date	Mintage	F12	VF20	XF40	MS60	MS63
1990(l)	12,000	PF60 875				

Y# 678 25 ROUBLES (Page 74)
173.29 g., 0.900 Silver 5.0143 oz. ASW, 60 mm. **Subject:** Bolshoi Theater 225 Years **Obv:** Double-headed eagle **Rev:** Dancing couple scene **Edge:** Reeded **Note:** Illustration reduced.

Date	Mintage	F12	VF20	XF40	MS60	MS63
2001	2,000	PF65 350				

Y# A387 100 ROUBLES (Page 52)
1111.12 g., 0.900 Silver 32.151 oz. ASW, 100 mm. **Subject:** WWII Victory **Rev:** Allied Commanders

Date	Mintage	F12	VF20	XF40	MS60	MS63
1995	1,500	PF63 1,400		PF65 1,600		

Y# 488 100 ROUBLES (Page 55)
1111.09 g., 0.900 Silver 32.150 oz. ASW, 100 mm. **Subject:** Ballet - Nutcracker **Obv:** Double-headed eagle **Rev:** Marsha cradling nutcracker doll

Date	Mintage	F12	VF20	XF40	MS60	MS63
1996	1,000	PF63 1,300		PF65 1,500		

SAMOA
(formerly Western Samoa)

KM# 120 2 TALA (Page 63)
42.41 g., 0.925 Silver 1.2614 oz. ASW **Obv:** National arms **Rev:** Value and three scenes **Note:** Part of a tri-national, three-coin matching set with Cook Islands and Fiji.

Date	Mintage	F12	VF20	XF40	MS60	MS63
1998	Est. 20000	PF63 50.00				

KM# 115 5 TALA (Page 59)
15.55 g., 0.925 Silver 0.4625 oz. ASW **Subject:** War and peace **Obv:** National arms **Rev:** Arrows and sword **Note:** 1/2 of 2-part coin, combined with Kiribati KM#22, issued in sets only. Value is determined by combining the 2 parts.

Date	Mintage	F12	VF20	XF40	MS60	MS63
ND(1997)	Est. 10000	PF63 28.00				

KM# 62 25 TALA (Page 19)
155.50 g., 0.999 Silver 4.9944 oz. ASW, 65 mm. **Subject:** Kon-Tiki **Obv:** National arms **Rev:** Sailing ship **Note:** Illustration reduced.

Date	Mintage	F12	VF20	XF40	MS60	MS63
1986	—	PF63 175	PF65 200			

SAN MARINO

KM# 494 2 EURO (Page 113)
8.50 g., Bi-Metallic Nickel-Brass center in Copper-Nickel ring, 25.75 mm. **Subject:** Sandra Botticeli, 500th Anniversary of Death

Date	Mintage	F12	VF20	XF40	MS60	MS63
2010R	130,000	—	—	—	45.00	55.00

SIERRA LEONE

KM# 78 10 DOLLARS (Page 59)
28.28 g., 0.925 Silver 0.841 oz. ASW **Subject:** Diana - The Peoples' Princess **Obv:** Arms **Rev:** Diana with Mother Theresa

Date	Mintage	F12	VF20	XF40	MS60	MS63
1997	Est. 10000	PF60 42.50				

SINGAPORE

KM# 166 250 DOLLARS (Page 63)
31.10 g., 0.999 Gold 0.999 oz. AGW **Subject:** Year of the Tiger **Obv:** Arms with supporters **Rev:** Stylized tiger

Date	Mintage	F12	VF20	XF40	MS60	MS63
1998	6,800	PF60 BV+10%				

SLOVAKIA

KM# 102 2 EURO (Page 109)
8.50 g., Bi-Metallic Nickel-Brass center in Copper-Nickel ring, 25.75 mm. **Obv:** Double cross on middle of three hills **Rev:** Value at left, expanded map of European Union at left

Date	Mintage	F12	VF20	XF40	MS60	MS63
2009	39,250,000	—	—	—	5.00	6.00
2009	13,300	PF63 25.00				

SOUTH AFRICA

KM# 181 RAND (Pages 57,58)
15.00 g., 0.925 Silver 0.4461 oz. ASW, 32.7 mm. **Subject:** Women of South Africa **Obv:** Protea flower **Rev:** Stylized 1/2 head facing within map **Edge:** Reeded

Date	Mintage	F12	VF20	XF40	MS60	MS63	MS65
1997	3,312	—				25.00	30.00
1997	2,329	PF65 40.00					

KM# 182 RAND (Page 60)
3.11 g., 0.9999 Gold 0.100 oz. AGW, 16.5 mm. **Subject:** 30th Anniversary - First Heart Transplant **Obv:** National arms. **Legend:** SOUTH AFRICA **Rev:** Doctor working on stylized heart **Edge:** Reeded

Date	Mintage	F12	VF20	XF40	MS60	MS63
1997	1,000	PF65 200				

KM# 145 2 RAND (Page 40)
33.63 g., 0.925 Silver 1.000 oz. ASW, 38.7 mm. **Subject:** Coin Minting **Obv:** National arms **Rev:** Assorted coins and design above value **Edge:** Reeded **Note:** 50 pieces used in jewelry mountings.

Date	Mintage	F12	VF20	XF40	MS60	MS63
1992	6,738	PF60 50.00	PF63 55.00	PF65 65.00		

KM# 511 50 RAND (Page 117)
15.55 g., 0.9999 Gold 0.500 oz. AGW, 27 mm.

Date	Mintage	F12	VF20	XF40	MS60	MS63
2011	—	PF65 975				

KM# 474 100 RAND (Pages 106,108)
31.11 g., 0.999 Gold 0.9991 oz. AGW, 32.7 mm. **Obv:** White rhino silouette and forepart **Rev:** Rhino standing facing within large silhouette

Date	Mintage	F12	VF20	XF40	MS60	MS63
2009	4,000	PF65 1,900				

SPAIN

KM# 911 2000 PESETAS
26.70 g., 0.925 Silver 0.794 oz. ASW **Ruler:** Juan Carlos I **Subject:** Olympics **Obv:** Conjoined busts of King and Crown Prince right **Rev:** Tug-of-war

Date	Mintage	F12	VF20	XF40	MS60	MS63
1992	9,043	—	—	—	—	65.00
1992	33,980	PF63 60.00	PF65 70.00			

Note: Uncirculated strikes have medallic die alignment and edges with reeded and plain sections; Proof strikes have coin die alignment and reeded edges

KM# 839 5000 PESETAS (Page 30)
54.00 g., 0.925 Silver 1.6059 oz. ASW **Ruler:** Juan Carlos I **Subject:** Discovery of America **Obv:** Crowned shield flanked by pillars with banner within beaded circle **Rev:** Santa Maria

Date	Mintage	F12	VF20	XF40	MS60	MS63
1989	23,630	—	—	—	—	60.00
1989	32,799	PF63 75.00				

KM# 1052 10 EURO (Page 84)
27.00 g., 0.925 Silver 0.803 oz. ASW, 40 mm. **Ruler:** Juan Carlos I **Obv:** Head left **Rev:** Sailing ship - De Elcano **Edge:** Reeded

Date	Mintage	F12	VF20	XF40	MS60	MS63
2003	12,486	PF63 75.00	PF65 90.00			

SWITZERLAND

KM# 66 5 FRANCS (Page 23)
13.20 g., Copper-Nickel, 31.45 mm. **Subject:** 100th Anniversary - Birth of Le Corbusier **Obv:** Value within diamond shape **Rev:** Standing figure within squared design **Edge Lettering:** DOMINUS PROVIDEBIT (13 stars)

Date	Mintage	F12	VF20	XF40	MS60	MS63
1987B	960,000	—	—	—	8.00	12.00
1987B	62,515	**PF60** 17.00				

KM# 67 5 FRANCS (Page 25)
13.20 g., Copper-Nickel, 31.45 mm. **Subject:** Olympics - Dove and Rings **Obv:** Value within entwined circles **Rev:** Stylized dove and circles **Edge Lettering:** DOMINUS PROVIDEBIT (13 stars)

Date	Mintage	F12	VF20	XF40	MS60	MS63
1988B	1,026,000	—	—	—	8.00	12.00
1988B	68,527	**PF60** 16.00				

UKRAINE

KM# 85 10 HRYVEN (Page 67)
33.90 g., 0.925 Silver 1.0082 oz. ASW, 38.6 mm. **Subject:** Birth of Jesus **Obv:** National arms, value and angels **Rev:** Nativity scene **Edge:** Reeded

Date	Mintage	F12	VF20	XF40	MS60	MS63
1999	10,000	**PF65** 400				

UNITED STATES

KM# 368 5 CENTS (Page 90)
Jefferson - Westward Expansion - Lewis & Clark Bicentennia
5.00 g., **Copper-Nickel**, 21.2 mm. **Obv. Designer:** Joe Fitzgerald and Don Everhart II **Rev. Designer:** Jamie Franki and Norman E. Nemeth **ObvDesc:** Thomas Jefferson large profile right; **RevDesc:** American Bison right

Date	Mintage	MS65	Prf65
2005P	448,320,000	1.50	—
2005P Satin Finish	1,160,000	4.00	—
2005D	487,680,000	1.50	—
2005D Satin Finish	1,160,000	4.00	—
2005S	3,344,679	—	6.50

KM# 295 25 CENTS
50 State Quarters - New Jersey 5.67 g., **Copper-Nickel Clad Copper**, 24.3 mm.

Date	Mintage	MS63	MS65	Prf65
1999P	363,200,000	1.00	5.00	—
1999D	299,028,000	1.00	4.00	—
1999S	3,713,359	—	—	3.50

KM# 320 25 CENTS (Page 76)
50 State Quarters - Rhode Island 5.67 g., **Copper-Nickel Clad Copper**, 24.3 mm.

Date	Mintage	MS63	MS65	Prf65
2001P	423,000,000	0.80	5.50	—
2001D	447,100,000	0.80	6.00	—
2001S	3,094,140	—	—	4.00

KM# 332 25 CENTS (Page 78)
50 State Quarters – Ohio 5.67 g., **Copper-Nickel Clad Copper**, 24.3 mm.

Date	Mintage	MS63	MS65	Prf65
2002P	217,200,000	0.80	5.50	—
2002D	414,832,000	0.80	5.50	—
2002S	3,084,245	—	—	2.30

KM# 372 25 CENTS (Page 92)
50 State Quarters – Oregon 5.67 g., **Copper-Nickel Clad Copper**, 24.3 mm.

Date	Mintage	MS63	MS65	Prf65
2005P	316,200,000	0.65	5.00	—
2005P Satin Finish	Inc. above	1.50	4.50	—
2005D	404,000,000	0.65	5.00	—
2005D Satin Finish	Inc. above	1.50	4.50	—
2005S	3,262,960	—	—	2.30

KM# 382 25 CENTS (Page 94)
50 State Quarters – Nevada 5.67 g., **Copper-Nickel Clad Copper**, 24.3 mm.

Date	Mintage	MS63	MS65	Prf65
2006P	277,000,000	0.65	5.00	—
2006P Satin Finish	Inc. above	1.50	4.50	—
2006D	312,800,000	0.65	5.00	—
2006D Satin Finish	Inc. above	1.50	4.50	—
2006S	2,862,078	—	—	2.30

KM# 546 25 CENTS (Page 129)
America the Beautiful - Mount Rushmore National Memorial 5.67 g., **Copper-Nickel Clad Copper**, 24.3 mm. **Rev. Designer:** Joseph Menna

Date	Mintage	MS63	MS65	Prf65
2013P	231,800,000	0.75	5.00	—
2013D	272,400,000	0.75	5.00	—
2013S	920,695	—	7.50	—
2013S	—	—	—	3.75

KM# 208 HALF DOLLAR (Pages 6,7)
George Washington, 250th Birth Anniversary. **ObvDesc:** George Washington on horseback facing **RevDesc:** Mount Vernon, 12.50 g., 0.900 Silver 0.3617 oz. ASW. **Obv. Designer:** Elizabeth Jones **Rev. Designer:** Matthew Peloso

Date	Mintage	MS65	Prf65
1982D	2,210,458	13.70	—
1982S	4,894,044	—	13.70

KM# 262 HALF DOLLAR (Page 50)
1996 Atlanta Olympics - Baseball. **ObvDesc:** Baseball batter at plate, catcher and umpire • **RevDesc:** Hemisphere and Atlanta Olympics logo • 11.34 g., **Copper-Nickel Clad Copper** • **Obv. Designer:** Edgar Z. Steever • **Rev. Designer:** T. James Ferrell

Date	Mintage	MS65	Prf65
1995S	164,605	19.50	—
1995S	118,087	—	17.50

KM# 209 DOLLAR (Pages 9,10)
1984 Los Angeles Olympics - Discus. **ObvDesc:** Tripled discus thrower and five star logo **RevDesc:** Eagle bust left, 26.73 g., 0.900 Silver 0.7734 oz. ASW. **Obv. Designer:** Elizabeth Jones

Date	Mintage	MS65	Prf65
1983P	294,543	34.80	—
1983D	174,014	34.70	—
1983S	174,014	34.80	—
1983S	1,577,025	—	36.80

KM# 210 DOLLAR (Page 13)
1984 Los Angeles Olympics - Stadium Statues. **ObvDesc:** Statues at exterior of Los Angeles Memorial Coliseum **RevDesc:** Eagle standing on rock, 26.73 g., 0.900 Silver 0.7734 oz. ASW. **Obv. Designer:** Robert Graham

Date	Mintage	MS65	Prf65
1984P	217,954	34.80	—
1984D	116,675	35.30	—
1984S	116,675	35.30	—
1984S	1,801,210	—	36.80

KM# 220 DOLLAR (Page 22)
Constitution Bicentennial. **ObvDesc:** Feather pen and document **RevDesc:** Group of people, 26.73 g., 0.900 Silver 0.7734 oz. ASW. **Obv. Designer:** Patricia L. Verani

Date	Mintage	MS65	Prf65
1987P	451,629	34.80	—
1987S	2,747,116	—	36.80

KM# 222 DOLLAR (Page 25)
1988 Olympics. **ObvDesc:** Olympic torch and Statue of Liberty torch within laurel wreath • **RevDesc:** Olympic rights within olive wreath • 26.73 g., 0.900 Silver 0.7734 oz. ASW. • **Obv. Designer:** Patricia L. Verani • **Rev. Designer:** Sherl Joseph Winter

Date	Mintage	MS65	Prf65
1988D	191,368	34.80	—
1988S	1,359,366	—	36.80

KM# 236 DOLLAR (Page 38)
White House Bicentennial. **ObvDesc:** White House's north portico **RevDesc:** John Hoban bust left, main entrance doorway, 26.73 g., 0.900 Silver 0.7734 oz. ASW. **Obv. Designer:** Edgar Z. Steever **Rev. Designer:** Chester Y. Martin

Date	Mintage	MS65	Prf65
1992D	123,803	37.80	—
1992W	375,851	—	38.80

KM# 249 DOLLAR (Page 46)
Thomas Jefferson 250th Birth Anniversary. **ObvDesc:** Jefferson's head left **RevDesc:** Monticello home, 26.73 g., 0.900 Silver 0.7734 oz. ASW.

Date	Mintage	MS65	Prf65
1993P	266,927	36.80	—
1993S	332,891	—	40.80

KM# 268 DOLLAR (Page 55)
1996 Atlanta Paralympics - Wheelchair racer. **ObvDesc:** Wheelchair racer approaching with uplifted arms **RevDesc:** Atlanta Olympics logo, 26.73 g., 0.900 Silver 0.7734 oz. ASW. **Obv. Designer:** James C. Sharpe and Alfred F. Maletsky **Rev. Designer:** Thomas D. Rogers, Sr.

Date	Mintage	MS65	Prf65
1996D	14,497	305	—
1996P	84,280	—	71.00

KM# 298 DOLLAR (Page 68)
Dolley Madison. **ObvDesc:** Madison bust right, at left **RevDesc:** Montpelier home, 26.73 g., 0.900 Silver 0.7734 oz. ASW. **Obv. Designer:** Tiffany & Co. and T. James Ferrell **Rev. Designer:** Tiffany & Co. and Thomas D. Rogers, Sr.

Date	Mintage	MS65	Prf65
1999P	22,948	38.30	—
1999P	158,247	—	38.30

KM# 313 DOLLAR (Pages 69,70)

Leif Ericson. **ObvDesc:** Ericson bust helmeted right **RevDesc:** Viking ship sailing left, 26.73 g., 0.900 **Silver** 0.7734 oz. ASW. **Obv. Designer:** John Mercanti **Rev. Designer:** T. James Ferrell

Date	Mintage	MS65	Prf65
2000P	28,150	69.00	—
2000P	58,612	—	62.50

KM# 310 DOLLAR (Page 70)

8.07 g., **Copper-Zinc-Manganese-Nickel Clad Copper**, 26.5 mm. **Obv. Designer:** Glenda Goodacre **Rev. Designer:** Thomas D. Rodgers **ObvDesc:** Sacagawea bust right, with baby on back **RevDesc:** Eagle in flight left

Date	Mintage	MS63	MS65	Prf65
2000P	767,140,000	2.00	7.50	—
2000P Goodacre Presentation	5,000	—	575	—
2000D	518,916,000	2.00	11.00	—
2000D from Millennium Set	5,500	10.00	50.00	—
2000S	4,048,000	—	—	5.00

KM# 325 DOLLAR (Page 74)

Native American - Bison. **ObvDesc:** Native American bust right **RevDesc:** Bison standing left, 26.73 g., 0.900 **Silver** 0.7734 oz. ASW.

Date	Mintage	MS65	Prf65
2001D	197,131	165	—
2001P	272,869	—	169

KM# 338 DOLLAR (Page 80)

U.S. Military Academy at West Point -Bicentennial. **ObvDesc:** Cadet Review flagbearers, Academy buildings in background **RevDesc:** Academy emblems - Corinthian helmet and sword, 26.73 g., 0.900 **Silver** 0.7734 oz. ASW. **Obv. Designer:** T. James Ferrell **Rev. Designer:** John Mercanti

Date	Mintage	MS65	Prf65
2002W	103,201	38.30	—
2002W	288,293	—	39.80

KM# 362 DOLLAR (Page 86)

Thomas A. Edison - Electric Light 125th Anniversary. **ObvDesc:** Edison half-length figure facing holding light bulb **RevDesc:** Light bulb and rays, 23.73 g., 0.900 **Silver** 0.6866 oz. ASW. **Obv. Designer:** Donna Weaver **Rev. Designer:** John Mercanti

Date	Mintage	MS65	Prf65
2004P	68,031	40.80	—
2004P	213,409	—	41.80

KM# 376 DOLLAR (Pages 89,92)

U.S. Marine Corps, 230th Anniversary. **ObvDesc:** Flag Raising at Mt. Suribachi on Iwo Jima **RevDesc:** Marine Corps emblem, 26.73 g., 0.900 **Silver** 0.7734 oz. ASW. **Obv. Designer:** Norman E. Nemeth **Rev. Designer:** Charles Vickers

Date	Mintage	MS65	Prf65
2005P	130,000	48.00	—
2005P	370,000	—	52.50

KM# 388 DOLLAR (Page 94)

Benjamin Franklin, 300th Birth Anniversary. **ObvDesc:** Bust 3/4 right, signature in oval below **RevDesc:** Continental Dollar of 1776 in center, 26.73 g., 0.900 **Silver** 0.7734 oz. ASW. **Obv. Designer:** Don Everhart II **Rev. Designer:** Donna Weaver

Date	Mintage	MS65	Prf65
2006P	58,000	40.80	—
2006P	142,000	—	51.00

KM# 401 DOLLAR (Page 99)

Presidents - George Washington, 8.07 g., **Copper-Zinc-Manganese-Nickel Clad Copper**, 26.5 mm. **Obv. Designer:** Joseph Menna **Rev. Designer:** Don Everhart **Edge Lettering:** IN GOD WE TRUST date, mint mark E PLURIBUS UNUM **Notes:** Date and mint mark incuse on edge. **ObvDesc:** Bust 3/4 facing left **RevDesc:** Statue of Liberty

Date	Mintage	MS63	MS65	Prf65
2007P	176,680,000	2.00	3.00	—
2007P Satin Finish	895,628	2.00	4.00	—
(2007) Plain edge error	Inc. above	175	275	—
2007D	163,680,000	2.00	3.00	—
2007D Satin Finish	895,628	2.00	4.00	—
2007S	3,883,103	—	—	3.00

KM# 405 DOLLAR (Page 99)

Jamestown - 400th Anniversary. **ObvDesc:** Two settlers and Native American **RevDesc:** Three ships, 26.73 g., 0.900 **Silver** 0.7734 oz. ASW. **Obv. Designer:** Donna Weaver and Don Everhart II **Rev. Designer:** Susan Gamble and Charles Vickers

Date	Mintage	MS65	Prf65
2007P	79,801	40.80	—
2007P	258,802	—	38.30

KM# 418 DOLLAR (Page 101)

Central High School Desegregation. **ObvDesc:** Children's feet walking left with adult feet in military boots **RevDesc:** Little Rock's Central High School, 26.73 g., 0.900 **Silver** 0.7734 oz. ASW. **Obv. Designer:** Richard Masters and Charles Vickers **Rev. Designer:** Don Everhart II

Date	Mintage	MS65	Prf65
2007P	66,093	40.80	—
2007P	124,618	—	43.00

KM# 439 DOLLAR (Page 103)

American Bald Eagle. **ObvDesc:** Eagle with flight, mountain in background at right **RevDesc:**

Great Seal of the United States 26.73 g., 0.900 **Silver** 0.7734 oz. ASW. **Obv. Designer:** Joel Iskowitz and Don Everhart II **Rev. Designer:** James Licaretz

Date	Mintage	MS65	Prf65
2008P	110,073	44.00	—
2008P	243,558	—	38.30

KM# 221 FIVE DOLLAR (Page 22)

Constitution Bicentennial. **ObvDesc:** Eagle left with quill pen in talon **RevDesc:** Upright quill pen 8.36 g., 0.900 **Gold** 0.2419 oz. AGW.

Date	Mintage	MS65	Prf65
1987W	214,225	442	—
1987W	651,659	—	442

KM# 239 FIVE DOLLAR (Page 39)

Columbus Quincentenary. **ObvDesc:** Columbus' profile left, at right, map of Western Hemisphere at left **RevDesc:** Arms of Spain, and parchment map 8.36 g., 0.900 **Gold** 0.2419 oz. AGW. • **Obv. Designer:** T. James Ferrell **Rev. Designer:** Thomas D. Rogers, Sr.

Date	Mintage	MS65	Prf65
1992W	24,329	442	—
1992W	79,730	—	442

KM# 215 FIVE DOLLAR (Pages 18,19)

Statue of Liberty Centennial. **ObvDesc:** Statue of Liberty head right **RevDesc:** Eagle in flight left, 8.36 g., 0.900 **Gold** 0.2419 oz. AGW.

Date	Mintage	MS65	Prf65
1986W	95,248	442	—
1986W	404,013	—	442

KM# 286 100 DOLLAR (Page 58)

RevDesc: Eagle in flight over sun rise 31.11 g., 0.9995 **Platinum** 0.9995 oz. APW, 33 **Obv. Designer:** John Mercanti **Rev. Designer:** Thomas D. Rogers Sr **ObvDesc:** Statue of Liberty **RevDesc:** Eagle in flight over sun rise

Date	Mintage	MS65	Prf65
1997W	15,885	—	1,422
1997	56,000	1,385	—

For more than 30 years,

Krause Publications has been proud to honor
the best in numismatic design, artistic vision,
and extraordinary craftsmanship through the
Coin of the Year Awards.

   Conceived by Krause Publications' founder
Chester "Chet" Krause and former President
and CEO Clifford "Cliff" Mishler, the
Coin of the Year took root in 1984, and has
since evolved into an international symbol of
accomplishment and recognition of numismatic
creativity.

   Please join us in celebrating the notable
efforts and execution of mints, artisans, and
inspired numismatists worldwide in this well
deserved salute to excellence.

COIN OF THE YEAR
by krause publications

kp **krause publications**
A DIVISION OF F+W, A Content + eCommerce Company
www.shopnumismaster.com